PRAISE FOR *THE E-FACTOR*

"Business as usual? Not anymore. Adrie and Marion have created a 'must-read' guide for entrepreneurs who want to compete effectively in today's business environment. Learn how to go beyond the tried-and-true to catapult your business to success."

—SUSAN WILSON SOLOVIC, CEO, It's Your Biz

"The mix of traditional and online tactics provided me with much food for thought. So often I see colleagues forgoing some of the long-standing traditional channels for networking and engaging with potential clients, colleagues, and talent. Here, Adrie and Marion have illustrated how the two worlds of entrepreneurship—the traditional and the new ages of networking—can intersect for an even higher level of connection, opportunity, and success. Many of the younger entrepreneurs out there should pick this book up so they can see how the traditional ways of engaging and networking are very much alive and valuable in today's global business environment."

—JIM SOLOMON,
Serial Entrepreneur; MBA Professor;
and Certified Public Accountant

THE

e

FACTOR

ENTREPRENEURSHIP IN
THE SOCIAL MEDIA AGE

ADRIE REINDERS &
MARION FREIJSEN

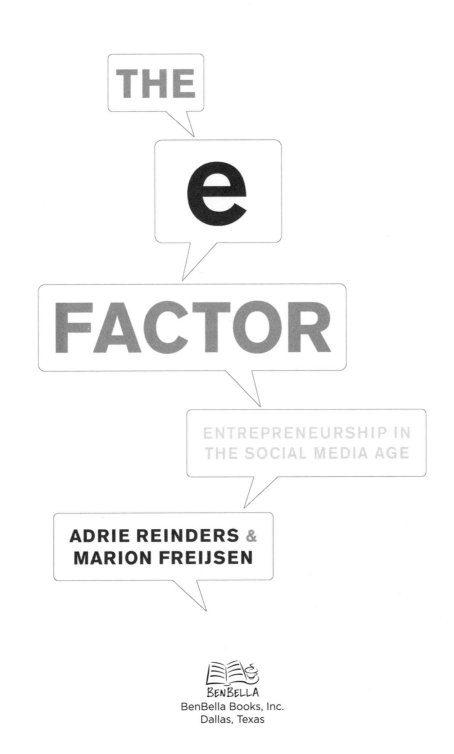

BenBella
BenBella Books, Inc.
Dallas, Texas

BenBella

BenBella Books, Inc.
10300 N. Central Expressway
Suite #400
Dallas, TX 75231
www.benbellabooks.com
Send feedback to feedback@benbellabooks.com

Printed in the United States of America
10 9 8 7 6 5 4 3 2 1

Library of Congress Cataloging-in-Publication Data is available for this title.
ISBN 978-1-935618-18-8

Editing by Erin Kelley
Copyediting by Deb Kirkby
Proofreading by Brittany Dowdle and Chris Gage
Cover design by Jarrod Taylor
Text design and composition by Neuwirth & Associates
Printed by Bang Printing

Distributed by Perseus Distribution
perseusdistribution.com

To place orders through Perseus Distribution:
Tel: 800-343-4499
Fax: 800-351-5073
E-mail: orderentry@perseusbooks.com

Significant discounts for bulk sales are available. Please contact Glenn Yeffeth at glenn@benbellabooks.com or (214) 750-3628.

We dedicate this book to Roeland Reinders, without whom we would never have started or even considered putting one toe across that finish line at the end of our journey.

CONTENTS

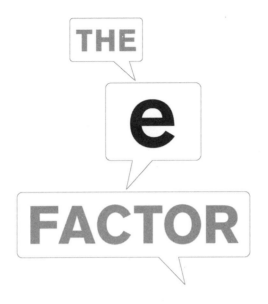

PROLOGUE

This book is for those who feel that they have a dream—be it a dream in its very earliest stages or one that's well developed and already taking shape in the world. It's for those with a dream to build a business from the ground up, who want to create something from scratch and turn it into something that they will leave behind as a legacy.

As serial entrepreneurs ourselves, we understand how hard the road to the fulfillment of that dream can be and how often you will feel a need for guidance and support. We know that it is a very lonely road to travel. On the other hand, we also understand how exhilarating it can be when you clear the obstacles that you face, and how amazing it will feel one day to look back and see how extremely far you have come.

We, the founders of EFactor.com, started together on our road to build the largest network for entrepreneurs. We are a team that is passionate about supporting and inspiring others to fulfill their own dreams of building and growing their own companies. We experienced obstacles just like any other entrepreneurs but always held close to our combined vision, drawing strength and inspiration from one another. As a team, you always support one another and ensure that you reach your goals, not individually but together. Our own journey with E Factor became the inspiration for this book—we want to share how solid you can be when you are part of a bigger group of like-minded people, people who understand the hardships and exhilarations of entrepreneurship and who will root for you every step of the way.

See this book as your guiding light; see it as the support on a bad day (or month or year) and understand that there are others out there who understand exactly who you are and what you are going through. We offer this information in the true spirit of collaboration and sharing that is entrepreneurship.

ADRIE REINDERS AND MARION FREIJSEN

INTRODUCTION
What Today's Entrepreneur Looks Like

Being an entrepreneur once was like walking the road less traveled. Nowadays, being an entrepreneur is like using the main line of a bustling metropolitan transit system. After forty years as entrepreneurs, we are happy to see that entrepreneurship has gained such notoriety.

Before society became so entrepreneur-friendly, many entrepreneurs worked alone for years. Those solo entrepreneurs may have succeeded, but many eventually recognized that there was strength in numbers—working together by sharing ideas, providing input and expertise, offering contacts and information when needed, and partnering to create new businesses. Today's entrepreneurial community serves as an energizing hub that brings together results already achieved and opportunities yet to come. As such, E Factor reflects the entrepreneurial movement and helps solidify the collaboration that can fuel entrepreneurial power to stimulate social benefits, economic wealth, and personal satisfaction for those of you with an idea and a passion to pursue.

As an entrepreneur, you are part of an exciting transition in the global environment. You are in position to shape the next decades of business. Although corporations are often floundering in this tough economic situation, you are actually seeing opportunities or may even be busier than ever. At the same time, however, you do see challenges and changes that are having an impact on what you could be doing. You might also be wondering how best to use the new tools at your disposal, like social media, social networking, mobile marketing, and mobile applications. And although you have your own set of rules and the passion to take chances and pursue your passions, you recognize the importance of considering the forces around you.

Although most people think they know how they look to outsiders, do you really understand how you compare to the entrepreneurs who came before you? Do you see yourself as the new model of entrepreneurship or do you share the same qualities as your predecessors? As this book will illustrate, no matter how innovative you are, you do share certain traits—drive, focus, creativity, discipline and passion—with those earlier entrepreneurs. You share most of the same qualities; however, that is not to say there are no differences. Like them, you are not afraid to bend the rules and think outside the box to achieve your goals. You are not burdened with the mindset of linear thinking. If there is a new way to create a product, interface with a client, or ship merchandise to market, you are among the first to embrace the concept just to see what happens. You have embraced technology and see the latest tools as the means to achieve your business dreams.

Thinking differently enables today's entrepreneurs to solve problems, develop ideas, and effectively use social media and networking to their advantage. If you ask some of the early entrepreneurs, they may even tell you that, thirty years ago, companies would have never believed they could communicate directly with their target consumers. Today's entrepreneur demands answers and will not accept the status quo. You thrive on the notion that there are no such things as problems—only challenges with solutions yet to be discovered. Does this sound like you?

The business world needs more like you. After all, it was entrepreneurs who brought consumers and business some of the best ideas we now often take for granted. Without the influential force of entrepreneurs like you, we would not have Facebook, Twitter, or E Factor; we would not be reading blogs; we would not have the iPhone or iPad; and we would not be buying all our merchandise on Amazon and then auctioning it off through eBay. That is why all of us need a better understanding of what defines entrepreneurship, how it is powered, and how it can be leveraged for even greater success for the business minds of today and those dreaming of joining the entrepreneurial ranks tomorrow.

In this introduction, you will learn more about what defines today's entrepreneur, including an overview of the trends and changes that we, as entrepreneurs ourselves, have seen over the last forty years. Your success will come from understanding how to combine the best traditional entrepreneurial thinking with the new tools, ideas, and channels now at your disposal. Before delving into the various tools and strategies, let's return to the roots of an entrepreneur to discover if an entrepreneur is born that way or if it's possible to become one.

THE ENTREPRENEURIAL MIND:
NATURE VS. NURTURE?

The idea of being an entrepreneur has really become a trend. Everyone wants to be one. Interestingly, more people think they are entrepreneurs than truly are—some are simply business owners. Entrepreneurs truly are born, not made. You either have the innate ability to lead a startup and run your own business or you don't. There are challenges, obstacles, and pitfalls along the way; clearly, not everyone is equipped to or interested in navigating this road. Many are completely satisfied to work a set schedule and pick up their paycheck at the end of the week. If this is how you feel, then entrepreneurship might not be for you.

Although not everyone may share our opinion that entrepreneurs are born—much as in the old debate about leaders—our personal experiences drive our belief. As one of the authors of this book and a veteran entrepreneur, Adrie concluded that entrepreneurship had to be part of one's DNA. Six years ago, he discovered that the father he had grown up with was not his biological father. As he began to explore his new identity, he learned that his biological father was a business founder and entrepreneur. He found he had a half-brother and two nephews who were businessmen. Adrie's two sons are also businessmen. However, his adoptive family was not entrepreneurial and shared no interest in that type of career path. Suddenly, Adrie realized where he got his passion for entrepreneurship; it was in his blood. Now not all entrepreneurs have this type of experience or realization, but many do feel like this is what they were always meant to do.

In contrast, Marion's experiences demonstrate that many entrepreneurs might not be in touch with this biological connection to entrepreneurship. Marion spent more than twenty-five years in the corporate world. At one point, she handled five separate start-up companies in a row. However, throughout her time there, she did not feel as though she was a typical corporate employee. After reflecting on her work, Marion realized that, even though she was in a corporate environment and working for someone else, she was actually a silent entrepreneur and was approaching the work on these startups as though they were her own businesses and very successful ones at that. From there, albeit later in life, she migrated into the world of pure entrepreneurship, with a newfound realization that she had always been an entrepreneur—a serial entrepreneur, actually—at heart. As our business now shows us, anyone can encourage his or her internal entrepreneur to emerge.

ENTREPRENEURS ABOUND

Now, let's take a further look at what it takes to bring this hidden entrepreneur into the open and activate the traits necessary to leverage the entrepreneurial spirit. Some excellent examples come to mind, such as Brian Scudamore, who started 1-800-GOT-JUNK in 1989 with $700 just after finishing high school. He had a vision of what he wanted to do, but he also was willing to take a risk to see it become a reality. He took the risk by hiring other people and helping them share in his vision. Brian wanted to make trash look good, so he created an image of a professional service with drivers in uniforms, clear pricing, clean trucks, and reliable and friendly service. Brian realized early on that technology would play a role in what he wanted to achieve, so he took a chance on using a call center format to standardize the business practice and keep service moving smoothly. This approach would also help when scaling up the number of franchise locations. Now he has more than 220 franchise partners in the United States, Canada, and Australia.

Consider Perez Hilton, who went from coffee shop blogger to the Queen of All Media. Starting off with an idea, a laptop, and a drink in a Hollywood coffee shop, Perez Hilton started out with only a basic knowledge of blogging software and an idea about how to turn a profit from blogging. The site has grown through the power of social media and his wicked wit for capturing and questioning "everything celebrity." Now he is his own media empire. He sells millions of dollars' worth of advertising on his blog, writes books, hosts events, and created his own brand. Perez Hilton was offered upwards of $20 million for the rights to his blog. To date, he continues to perch atop a pink empire that keeps growing and adding new ideas, including representing new artists and his own record label.

Finally, there are "mompreneurs" like Sari Crevin of BooginHead. She proved that you don't need to have a lot of fancy credentials to be an entrepreneur and make seven figures while working for yourself on a part-time basis. She went with what she knew best—being a mom—and dealing with some messy situations. That's not to say she did not do her time in the corporate world. Once upon a time, she worked in human resources management for Microsoft. Because she could not find a product that fit her needs, she decided it was time to develop her own. Now with sales in the millions, her company sells attachable hooks and related products for the sippy cups and pacifiers that often serve as projectiles among the younger set. She credits a network of other mompreneurs in helping her start a company and get past all the hurdles along the way.

THE FACE OF A NEW GENERATION

All of these examples point to the diverse faces of the new generation of entrepreneurs. Today's entrepreneur is younger, faster, stronger, and more willing to take risks at a younger age. The idea that anyone at any age could be an entrepreneur was virtually unheard of thirty or forty years ago. Although some unique individuals ventured out on their own to start a business—a restaurant or local business—there were not global entrepreneurs or young upstarts forgoing the corporate world completely in favor of striking it rich or making a world of difference. Young people today are fearless and willing to take chances at an even younger age, encouraged by parents, friends, and mentors. They do not wonder if they can dream of being a star; television shows and other success stories of young people as entrepreneurs tell them that anything is possible.

This may have to do with the fact that they are more tuned in to the world around them thanks to technology. Those raised on a steady diet of Internet, media, and social networking have a very different perspective than those who did not have access to the same amount of information delivered regularly to them through their smartphones and laptops. The level and frequency of information has sped up time for young entrepreneurs, who are used to a world of instant answers and a dizzying array of products that cater to them. It is no wonder that they do not think anything is impossible when, every day, they see new things and new opportunities that engage and delight them.

TECHNOLOGY MAKES THE HEART GROW FONDER

Behind the face of the new entrepreneur is the driving force of technology that tells you that you can work in new and different ways than perhaps any entrepreneur who came before you. Thanks to technological advancements, the globe is shrinking and access to people you might have never met or done business with before is growing. This new technology has created an international landscape where your suppliers do not have to be within commuting distance. Now it is not uncommon to ship products halfway around the world. China has become the leader in manufacturing and, with the advances in technology, it is simply a matter of interfacing online to conduct business, move commerce, or order supplies.

The same can be said for how technology opens up a new world for entrepreneurs to tap into talent, funding, networking, and clientele. Whether it is through online directories, online advertising, or online social networking, technology has linked people together to share ideas, collaborate on projects, share resources, and start businesses. People who might otherwise never have met or crossed paths in the business world just a few decades ago are now finding each other and working together in new and exciting ways. Technology has opened up such roles as outsourcing, freelancing, contract workers, and telecommuting.

Having these opportunities means that companies are learning to work differently in terms of how they spend money and acquire talent. And among those to pioneer such concepts and roles are today's entrepreneurs, who recognized early on what they could do with technology. Technology has also changed an entrepreneur's ability to locate key personnel within an organization. For example, with social media, it is easier than ever to find the correct department or the head of shipping to facilitate business ventures. This channel has also helped to connect entrepreneurs to investors and mentors to help guide their business ideas to fruition.

However, despite the increasingly virtual nature of the world and the opportunity to create new relationships, today's entrepreneurs often still appreciate the traditional ways in which business has always been handled. That's why we can't stress enough how important it is to build business relationships. After more than forty years as entrepreneurs, we've found this principle is as true today as it was four decades ago. The only thing that might have changed is the way these relationships exist. Today's entrepreneurs can forge ahead by building long-term relationships without a physical meeting for months or years; others may never have a face-to-face meeting despite years of working together.

Yet these entrepreneurs have a lot to learn when it comes to understanding the personal touch points necessary to certain business relationships. Building face-to-face personal relationships with business associates is important. There will always be a need to feel people out on a human level to garner support for a business. Although, as long-standing entrepreneurs, we cannot be sure how practical having this one-on-one contact will be as time goes by, we still feel strongly that personal relationships are necessary for entrepreneurs to cultivate.

UNIVERSITY 101: RELEVANT?

As an entrepreneur, you may think that your traits and your tools will serve as your "get out of college or university jail" card. After all, so many entrepreneurs will tell you they never went or simply dropped out.

With so many entrepreneurs proudly proclaiming they became millionaires and billionaires without ever attending college or finishing a degree, it is easy to see why today's entrepreneurs may rebel against the notion that institutions of higher learning have any relevance to what they are trying to achieve. They believe they can get an education that will help them by living and working in the real world. Again, this is normal for the traditional entrepreneurial character, which expects instant results culled by taking shortcuts and having all the information and contacts they think they need at their fingertips. Despite all that, today's entrepreneur might want to reconsider skipping past university lessons.

Higher learning has caught on to the changes in the global business environment and many universities are altering their focus to offer courses that resonate with entrepreneurs, as well as to cover some very relevant aspects of leading a business. Entrepreneurs can glean skills that they might otherwise lack from these courses. Sure, there was a time when universities offered few or no classes on entrepreneurship. Guidance counselors did not suggest going out and starting your own business. Many who might have liked to have their own business, instead conformed to a traditional career path.

But today's students aren't forced to make that kind of sacrifice. Universities have made the leap into the current decade in terms of their thinking and approach to learning. Owning your own business is now talked about more readily, stoking the flames of entrepreneurship for the younger crowd. Colleges and universities are finally embracing entrepreneurship, creating undergraduate and graduate courses in the field. MIT and the University of California, Berkeley, are just a couple of the top universities now offering classes and graduate courses in entrepreneurship. Given the growing number of student loans but the lack of existing jobs, universities might have to do even more to attract young people as many decide to forgo higher education.

Instead, they will use the entrepreneurial force coursing through their veins simply to develop their own jobs by starting businesses, rather than hoping that a job awaits them upon graduation. As such, future generations of entrepreneurs are preparing earlier and more thoroughly for the rigors of today's business environment. With this comes a throwback to the idea that the education system can prepare entrepreneurs to be more effective in their role, whether it is through a brick-and-mortar university or through e-learning techniques now being developed to appeal to their character.

BRIDGING THE ENTREPRENEURIAL GAP

Comparing the young entrepreneur preparing today to those of us with forty years of experience in entrepreneurship, there are differences but there are also many similarities. That is why we are using this book as a way to bridge the entrepreneurial gap. Within each chapter, you will see that today's entrepreneurs must consider how to leverage traditional business principles (old rules), as well as modern technology, tools, and channels (new rules) to be successful in the modern global business environment. Our own experiences as longtime entrepreneurs have shown us that it is critical to employ both old and new rules to jump ahead of the competition and leap over the challenges along the way.

For us, it is really nothing new. Adrie was an original entrepreneur. Having left school at age sixteen, he continued another sixteen years of night school to complete his education and began building successful businesses as he went. Back then, there were no support groups or organizations where entrepreneurs got together. What is different today is that the newer generations of entrepreneurs are much better equipped to handle the challenges and forces within the global business environment. They have a box of tools to navigate the often murky waters of the global business environment. However, within this environment, perils are also lurking that can compromise the reputation or growth potential of a business, especially when using some of those new tools, such as social media and mobile marketing, incorrectly. It is easy to be caught short by these when the typical behavior is to cut corners in hopes of becoming profitable quickly.

Instead, as this book will point out, we believe strongly in the notion that life experiences affect your business savvy. Your ability to bring your maturity and cognitive development into play when dealing with associates and clients can yield significant dividends. Success in entrepreneurship is not about learning a new skill or mastering a task; it is about being attuned to one's environment in order to know when it is time to capitalize on the situation and when it is time to hold back and ride out a particular storm. Things as simple as manners, respect, and integrity still go a long way in business—even today. Although passion and drive will always get you a certain way down the road, it is attention to these basic principles that will help you complete your course.

Despite knowing the new rules, it still pays to turn to a coach who has played by both sets of rules for a long time. Learn to recognize the value of wisdom that someone who has spent years on starting up businesses in all types of market cycles possesses.

A NEW REVOLUTION: E FACTOR

When we started E Factor, we had one goal in mind. We wanted to connect entrepreneurs of all ages and build a community where people could come together to exchange ideas, discuss problems, find solutions, and stimulate the growth of entrepreneurship. This was also a place where we could share our breadth of experience to shape a new generation of business professionals, empowering them with the tools of knowledge to build their success on their own terms. Although we saw ourselves as visionaries, even decades ago, we never predicted our ability to interface with so many entrepreneurs or participate and share our skills and knowledge with such a wide variety of entrepreneurs. This has been an exciting journey and one where we have captured many lessons and experiences along the way that we share through this book.

WHAT'S NEXT?

The book provides many examples and case studies on companies and entrepreneurs. Each chapter offers specific insights into various challenges and opportunities faced by today's entrepreneur where both old and new rules apply. A combination of tools and strategies is needed to soar over these hurdles and toward the ultimate goal you have in mind. Upcoming chapters address a variety of topics:

- The business environment is ever-changing with growing regulations, challenging finance sourcing, and new demands. The ever-increasing flow of information is moving at a pace that is hard to keep up with. This is in addition to the need for greater transparency in the market. What can you do?
- No matter what you do, good or bad, someone will post their reaction to it on the Internet and word of it will spread around the world. It requires more thought and planning before taking action—something that an entrepreneur did not have to think so much about just a decade or so ago; they could just act and worry about certain consequences later on. Do you have a plan?
- One of the most challenging aspects of startups today is funding. This is not the 1990s, where venture capitalists willingly invested money in any Internet startup or business-to-business (B2B) or business-to-consumer (B2C) venture. Today's global financial crisis has led to funding shortfalls and a long list of rules for what qualifies for funding. However, this new funding environment does not have to be

a challenge if today's entrepreneur implements the right strategies for funding. Where will you get the backing you need to fund your next great idea?

- The worlds of social media and social networking often become blurred and thought of as interchangeable when, in fact, there are specific differences. However, there are also tools that can be used for a wide range of business strategies and tasks. Social media can help in many areas of the business, including marketing and branding, reputation building, strategy and vision, financing and funding, new product development, and more. Do you know how to use it correctly?

- Despite the convenience and relevance of the virtual business world, there is still a need for events, physical handshakes and connections, and meetings to exchange ideas and develop relationships. Do you know how to communicate effectively in both worlds?

- Nowadays, you can work 24/7 on product development (outsourced to other countries) and you can share workflow and collaborate on new business ideas, get input and feedback, and transfer knowledge quickly through the virtual environment with Skype, cloud computing, etc. Yet, because of the technology, new demands and expectations have changed the speed at which you must operate. Can you leverage this new way of working?

- A new mindset is needed that builds on the traditional entrepreneurial mindset developed through a continual learning process, incorporating a long-term perspective, considering new expectations like integrating environmental and financial performance, social responsibility and an ever-changing set of consumer demands and interests. Is your mind ready?

- Even in the best-intentioned businesses, failure happens. In order to prevent failure for entrepreneurs, it is important to look at case studies where the business did not go as planned. How will you handle failure if it happens? Lessons can be learned from companies that failed at social media marketing like Walmart, Sony, and Skittles; other firms like Netflix can illustrate why it is so critical to know your audience and calculate all potential consequences of certain actions before you take them.

- Just as important as the failures are the success stories of companies on the move and why they succeeded. How can you incorporate lessons about others' successes? Learn about the traits of companies like Virgin America, ING, Fleet Feet, and more.

- Although there is a definite need for more entrepreneurs to kick off and actually start their own businesses (and the global economy is crying out for more businesses), education for entrepreneurs is still lacking and very few government initiatives actually help entrepreneurs. This requires a new vision for today's entrepreneur created by entrepreneurs. Can you bring this vision to life? All it takes is the willingness to share and collaborate.

This book provides key examples, stories, and tips for you as an entrepreneur to leverage the power of collaboration and sharing through E Factor and your network of fellow entrepreneurs to achieve your aspirations. We offer this information in the true spirit of collaboration and sharing that is entrepreneurship. Before we go any further, we would first like to share the story of our own entrepreneurial journey that led to E Factor.

THE E FACTOR STORY

THIS IS THE STORY of E Factor as told by its founders, Adrie and Marion. Together, along with their third partner, Roeland Reinders, they ran OHM Business Development, a company they started back in 2004. OHM focused on business development for young technology companies all over the world, focusing mainly on using the extensive network they had built to help these companies through the door of the Fortune 1500 at the highest possible level.

The personal introduction, combined with the trust between the individuals involved, meant that the three founders were able to help more than 250 companies achieve sales contracts and offer leads that the clients otherwise would have worked months to find—often nine to twelve months of building the connections that may eventually lead to a sale. It was also extremely interesting for Adrie and Marion to see how new startups worked.

Apart from their own experience in building companies from the ground up repeatedly throughout their careers, in this new business, Adrie and Marion found themselves getting a view of all these different companies—how they started their companies, how they handled issues, what those issues were, and how they approached every hurdle common among all the clients. This experience was in the back of their minds when they finished *The N Factor* in 2007, a book about networking that was also largely based on their OHM network experiences.

THE START OF E FACTOR

During the writing of that first book, Adrie and Marion decided to write a second book—more about entrepreneurship and the problem facing entrepreneurs globally—because they had learned so much about this while running OHM. The research for the second book (*this* book) led them to think about starting a community for entrepreneurs. At the time, *social networking* was an unknown term; instead, *community* was the common reference for what would become this virtual networking environment.

Back in 2007, Facebook was just beginning to become popular when Adrie and Marion were doing research for this book, but it did not have a professional emphasis. LinkedIn was in its early stages; in fact, the duo described LinkedIn in detail in *The N Factor*. In the time leading up to the conception of E Factor, both Marion and Adrie felt that the existing sites were lacking a number of things. The fledgling social networks seemed to lack a certain amount of functionality and purpose, especially in terms of assisting entrepreneurs and in providing practical support that would help them expand their networking abilities and grow their businesses. Adrie, Marion, and Roeland researched what entrepreneurs were looking for and what would help them achieve greater success. In the early stages of the writing process, Marion and Adrie spoke to many other entrepreneurs in order to get their perspectives.

Through this experience, they realized that no extensive online resources were available to entrepreneurs. Both were often asked questions about how to do one thing or another and entrepreneurs often sought their advice. The E Factor co-founders realized that a social media platform for entrepreneurs did not exist. So the team developed their "Four Pillars" on which they built E Factor. These four pillars basically answer four questions every single entrepreneur will deal with during their business' lifecycle:

1. How do I get funding?
2. How do I approach business development/networking?
3. How do I save money?
4. Where do I find knowledge, mentoring, and practical information?

E Factor was born out of a gap in the social networking market and a practical need for the enhancement of the entrepreneurial process.

CREATING E FACTOR

The first practical step in creating E Factor was to find some-one who could build the Web site itself. The founders knew that their Web site's focus had to be consumer interaction. However, $150,000 and six months later, the Web site still lacked the right type of interaction. The Web site instead was built for its aesthetic value and not for its function, even though they had emphasized the need for interaction as the primary functionality. At this point in time, the co-founders had a hard choice: either continue to work with the current web devel-oper and fix the existing site or start over completely. So they scrapped the existing site and started over.

It was back to square one. It was one of the most dif-ficult parts of the journey—there was still very little experi-ence that would translate directly into developing a real-time vehicle that would allow interaction and exchanges between members around the world. This time, they found a web developer through their own personal network who already had worked with another social network template. They started building and developing the Web site in a piecemeal fashion. This process may have been slower, but it ultimately allowed them to build a site that ran the way they had envi-sioned it and allowed them to control every step of the pro-cess. This second version of the Web site launched in March 2008, with updating and new development continuing even to this day. A completely new interface was finally launched in September 2010 and is represented in what the site looks like today.

FUNDING

A number of factors played a role in their decision on funding the organization. First of all, one has to look at what the expectation is regarding the long-term future of the organization. For E Factor, the team really wanted to look at an exit four years down the line, which involved either selling the company, going public, or merging with another company. This meant that to make it worthwhile for themselves and their investors, they would have to build the community substantially in that time frame and develop the site on an ongoing basis. The choice was to go for a large amount of funding (typically through a venture capitalist or financial institution) or raise money through wealthy individuals and private investors. The latter would be slower, in small chunks, but give more control of the organization and its development.

The choice was clear: E Factor would be supported by smaller investments, raised when needed—not giving up a chunk of ownership early on and diluting the investment of existing investors in the process. The fact that the economic crisis also occurred in those early months of the new site's development meant that it was a path that was chosen wisely—venture capitalist money was scarcely available for a long period of time and would have been hard to come by. An important advantage of the chosen route for funding was that, with every step of development of the site and the growth of the community (number of members), the value of the company increased. In this way, the founders raised $5 million or so over the past four years while controlling the majority of shares.

REFLECTIONS ON E FACTOR'S DEVELOPMENT

Adrie noted that they always had a very global vision for E Factor and that it was only a matter of time before the company spread around the world. When asked how much has changed since E Factor's start, Marion noted that, in principle, not that much was different. Essentially, the core ideas are very much still there. For instance, the concept of the Four Pillars still provides a very clear foundation of community for the Web site and the network.

One of the lessons that stands out for both Marion and Adrie is that you cannot necessarily trust everything you think you know. One of the problems for the social networking industry is that it has not been around for very long. That being said, there are few experts who definitively know what works and what does not work. The other problem is that what works today might not work tomorrow. The industry changes that quickly. This happened to both Marion and Adrie during the development of E Factor. At the beginning of E Factor, they received a lot of conflicting advice on how to do things. For example, they often got conflicting advice on how to set up the registration on the E Factor site. Some experts said that the registration process had to be very simple or people would not take the time to register at all. However, they found that if you have a registration process that is too simple, then you are left with no information on your members. Having comprehensive information on members is especially crucial for E Factor because we need to know things like where you are located in order to invite you to events in your area.

One of the aspects of E Factor that Marion and Adrie hold a lot of pride in is the fact that there is still a person behind the site. They feel that it is very important to provide member support. When E Factor members reach out for support, they often get it straight from the founders. The personal involvement that the founders still retain in the day-to-day activities of the site is a testament to their dedication to their work.

ADVICE AND COMMENTARY

After all of Adrie and Marion's experience as entrepreneurs, they are a cache of advice and knowledge. When asked what one piece of advice they would give to other entrepreneurs about using social networking, Marion was quick to answer. She said, "Help somebody else—answer someone else's question and then post your own!" This emphasis on the need for interaction on the E Factor site is an aspect of networking that both value. Given that the focus of their social networking site is simply as a place for entrepreneurs to interact, they feel very strongly about encouraging people actually to put themselves out there. Marion and Adrie also stressed the amount of work that it takes to start your own company. They both agreed that they underestimated the amount of time it takes to get it really right.

According to the founders, E Factor is the one place in the world where you can find a lot of different things for your business. It is the one place where entrepreneurs can get advice independently because it is provided by people who are entrepreneurs themselves, all working toward similar goals. It takes personalized advice to make an impact and truly help entrepreneurs and small-business owners. Although E Factor was created by the founders/entrepreneurs, it is not meant to be about them. Instead, they see themselves as mentors for several companies due to their passion for entrepreneurship.

Building a community like E Factor is a constant work in progress and shall never cease. It requires continuous feedback loops between members and the E Factor team itself in order to continue to grow and expand. It is just like building any other company—with the complicating factor here being that there are no paths laid out and everything is new and has to be discovered one item at a time. On a personal note, the E Factor founders faced their share of family and health issues during the four years the company was being built and developed— which has been the hardest part of building the company. Finding a good balance between what you face in your daily life and business and setting the right priorities is a hard nut to crack. Both Adrie and Marion always felt grateful that there were three founders—each willing to carry the other when and where necessary.

A NEW GAME:
OBSTACLES TO OVERCOME

AS ENTREPRENEURS, WE ALL work hard to build our business on a foundation of solid principles, great ideas, and accumulated knowledge. No matter how advanced technology gets, nothing can take the place of incredible and inventive ideas. The other thing that has remained the same is that many of the obstacles we faced more than thirty years ago are still here today. However, the way those challenges present themselves has changed a bit—there are new forces and factors at work, but there are also new tools and processes to address those challenges.

Obstacles or challenges have always been a part of business. Although they can slow you down and impede your progress, savvy entrepreneurs often see them as opportunities or situations where they can apply their knowledge or ideas to drive a new marketplace niche or open up a new business segment.

Now, you may ask how business is so different than it was twenty years ago. You come up with an idea, secure financing, and take your product to market. However, what underlies business decisions, actions, and results is the fact that the rules have changed. In actual fact, they are still changing. And if you are not prepared to address these changes, then you may stumble and actually fail to achieve your intended business goals and objectives.

Let's look at the challenges that are confronting today's entrepreneur as part of the new realities:

- Increased competition will have an impact on your ability to get noticed.
- Copycats infringe on your spotlight.
- Internet awareness can make or break you.
- Tightening regulations call for some unique solutions.
- Restricted resources require that you do more with much less.
- Talent and skills gaps leave many areas of your business underperforming.
- Financial limitations complicate getting your business up and running as fast as you want or even at all.

These are just some of the ways things are changing. Later chapters will touch on other game changers. However, the realities mentioned here are some of the largest hurdles today's entrepreneurs are facing as they look down the track toward the business start-up finish line. Getting up and running has truly become a marathon, requiring new training, strategies, and metrics for measuring performance. These changes also force entrepreneurs to evaluate and reassess their goals, products, and company structure constantly to meet the needs of this evolving business environment.

GAME ON: COMPETING WITH THE WORLD

Increased competition will have an impact on your ability to get noticed.

Gone are the days when you would only have to contend with one or two competitors because your business was operating within just one town or region. The Internet and global market have changed the landscape of business, offering you a world of potential customers. Yet, with that new audience come hundreds, sometimes thousands, of competitors on a daily basis. It might seem like our peers and colleagues are in direct competition with us as they have the same passion, drive, and talent to succeed as we do.

Instead of seeing competition as a problem for you and your business, look at it as an opportunity to get better. It is really about a challenge to see where you can make improvements that beat out this competition. It means finding more ways to be and do things differently—to attract and engage customers and to offer and market your solutions. This makes you constantly aware of the importance of staying on top of your game and motivating others involved in your business to bring their "A" game every day. Otherwise, the competition will stampede right over you unless you evolve and reinvent your business quickly.

We must constantly evolve as entrepreneurs and reinvent ourselves to stay current with market trends. Our creativity as entrepreneurs naturally leads us to discover solutions to problems. Here's what can help you gain leverage in the competitive environment:

- Be prepared to test yourself.
- View obstacles as opportunities.
- Meet your challenges head-on.
- Don't be afraid to reinvent your business plan.
- And remember, finding solutions is part of the job.

BUT THAT WAS MY IDEA!

Copycats infringe on your spotlight.

The power of the Internet cannot be ignored. It drives commerce. It redefines boundaries. It is one of the most influential forces in business today. And the Internet can make or break your business. One way it will break your business is through copycats. As an entrepreneur, you barely have the opportunity to take a product to market before a copycat has discovered your idea and is now flooding the market at the same time or even ahead of you.

This means that you have to stay three steps ahead of any copycats. Otherwise, they can:

- build your product cheaper;
- ship it to market faster; and
- become a stronger player in the industry before you even get out of bed tomorrow morning.

Therefore, your goal is to anticipate market trends and sidestep the competition by being aware of their tactics and developing a game plan to avert disaster. You must wrest control from the competition and be a driving force and innovator in your industry by using what you have—the characteristics of today's entrepreneur, like fast response, instant decision-making, and ingenuity to beat out the competition.

And, if your idea becomes the subject of copycats, then you have to work quickly to alter your product or service or, at the very least, find a way to spin it a different way and/or market it to a different audience. Whatever it takes, you need to make sure that your efforts did not go to waste because someone beat you to market. You start implementing a strategy immediately. After all, giving up is not a character trait of entrepreneurs.

This brings up issues of trust within an organization. You must carefully review and consistently check yourself to ensure control over information to your employees to avoid premature leaks via the Internet. Companies must carefully guard their projects with some very severe penalties if employees even breathe a hint of what might be in the works. Likewise, you have to ensure that business principles around control, leadership, and communication are enacted to keep a tight grip on your ideas, concepts, and products in development.

ALL THE INTERNET IS A STAGE . . . AND WE ARE MERELY PLAYERS

Internet awareness can make or break you.

Although some may copy us, another challenge might be that the transparency technology provides requires us to behave within a different framework. Increased technology has also played a role in adding to the new rules. As entrepreneurs and businesses, we are scrutinized as never before. The Internet has lifted the veil so that a whole range of stakeholders can now peer easily into our world. Although this has provided numerous ways to engage with stakeholders and to gather information and insight, it has led to new challenges never previously imagined. With more information now available than ever before and the ability to share it almost instantly, news about your company can quickly "go viral." And that can be quite sickening for your company if the news being transmitted is not good.

The Internet has changed the way businesses interface and not all of these changes have been positive. The eyes of the world are watching for you to make a misstep or miscalculation they can use to their advantage. Social media has laid bare many a company's soul, with many scrambling to address an employee's use of social media, clean up a tarnished brand image from bad news spread on the Internet, and use the Web to broadcast messages that address some sort of business crisis.

A wise entrepreneur anticipates and avoids potentially costly marketing and business mistakes, so careful thought is necessary before acting on any plans that your company is considering. All of your decisions—good and bad—will be broadcast around the world at the speed of light. This can be the death knell to start-up entrepreneurs who are not paying attention. Any negative comments must be dealt a counter-blow to soften or eliminate any criticism directed at your company. The weight can easily bury even the most successful start-up businesses.

Social media has opened the door to interface with customers like never before. The trick is to be proactive. We have seen companies that have a presence online without being active. They have "Contact Us" buttons to leave messages, but when consumers do so, their messages go unanswered. This is not using social media to its full potential. You must be an active partner with the consumer. Later chapters will address this challenge of being proactive when offering good news and in dealing with bad news.

TIGHTENING REGULATIONS: DELIVERING ON EXPECTATIONS

Tightening regulations call for some unique solutions.

As consumers become more aware of the impact companies can have on the environment, they are demanding changes to ensure the longevity of natural resources and the planet as a whole. We must be sensitive to consumers' concerns, especially in light of a groundswell of active conservation. Companies are now expected to report on their environmental performance in the same way they have been delivering reports on their financial performance. New rules are driven home by national and international regulations about greenhouse gas emissions, water conservation, and waste reduction—much of which was never a concern for an entrepreneur in the past.

Once, starting a business was simply about getting it set up and creating revenue and a sustainable profit. Now it is still about doing that but also about avoiding environmental damage. And if you are not doing it on your own, then ongoing regulatory pressures will force you into figuring out how to change your business plan and processes to meet these regulations.

Yet many entrepreneurs realized early on they do not have to trade off profits for corporate social responsibility and an increased regulatory environment. Many companies have actually thrived and gained a competitive edge by acting in a way that makes them stand out as admirable, socially responsible, and environmentally conscious companies. That effort has paid off handsomely as they have moved ahead in the marketplace by turning a challenge into an opportunity.

We have seen how consumers' ideals can shift during an economic downturn. There seems to be an increase in green thinking and corporate responsibility when the economy is growing. When there is prosperity, people have the opportunity to view their surroundings and to measure issues from a different perspective. They demand accountability. As entrepreneurs, you are on the front lines in preserving our environment for future generations. Together, we stand at the threshold of conservation and balancing jobs and growth with preservation.

Beyond the environmental challenge, new regulations about financial performance are an obstacle—but really another opportunity in disguise. Businesses must provide greater transparency in how money is spent and made. New accounting methods and government reporting regulations have intensified the responsibilities you feel as a business founder or owner. However, these need not be obstacles that slow you down. Arming yourself with the knowledge and understanding of what these regulations mean can help you adapt your business proactively. Again, entrepreneurs are flexible and think on their feet, so use these traits to your advantage when faced with an ever-increasing regulatory environment. Living up to those expectations only furthers your reputation and builds a following.

DOING MORE WITH LESS

Restricted resources require that you do more with much less.

The current business environment and economy are not offering a lot of help when it comes to resource availability. These are lean times. Funding is difficult to come by, and stakeholders are clamoring to trim the waste. These are not the days of old, when venture capitalists or banks handed entrepreneurs pots of money and told them to create a company based on any old idea. It is still okay to create a company from any old idea, but you will most likely have to go it alone. Although many would just throw up their hands and return to the corporate world, entrepreneurs should actually relish this opportunity.

After all, there are examples all over the world of entrepreneurs who started what are now booming, multimillion-dollar businesses for a few hundred or a few thousand dollars. Look at the case studies throughout this book, and you will see example after example of people who had no resources except themselves and turned their ideas into successes. They managed to find unique ways to get a business started with few or no resources. If anything, starting from next to nothing motivated them to think of how they could get the maximum return from what little they had. They continued to use this philosophy going forward, which helped them survive tough economic cycles. In contrast, those used to having an abundance of resources are now struggling because they never thought of making do with less as an opportunity. Companies that are "lean and mean" are actually the ones generating the most success.

Having fewer resources actually allows for greater efficiencies and less waste, which, in the long run, not only generates a higher level of productivity and performance but can also lead to greater profits. Again, this is another challenge or obstacle that becomes an opportunity. It is also one that illustrates how your attitude alters your perspective. Being a true entrepreneur means that you see these situations as ways to shape your business and build a competitive advantage rather than as something that could potentially slow you down.

FISHING IN THE TALENT POOL

Talent and skills gaps leave many areas of your business underperforming.

They say the talent pool is missing many fish, or at least fish that are fortified with the skills and knowledge necessary to help companies compete and win. As an entrepreneur who may be starting up a business, you too may be worried that you will not find the right people or that you personally do not have the right level of skill and knowledge to help your business perform at the level you want.

Although it may be true that your business has some talent and skills gaps, it is not because there is a shortfall in the school of fish in the world; you are just not using the right fish food to attract or keep the fish you need. You also might not be feeding yourself with the right training and learning mechanisms that could enhance your skill set and help your business achieve its true potential. This means taking action to incorporate ongoing learning practices to stimulate your own knowledge management system while also tending to anyone you have hired to help your business grow.

THE GLOBAL FINANCIAL SQUEEZE

Financial limitations make it difficult to get your business up and running as fast as you want or even at all.

The last few years have seen a tremendous decrease in banks willing to lend. Our global economy has been affected by a number of factors. As entrepreneurs, we face increasing difficulties in securing financing. Although this will be discussed in detail in the next chapter, let's focus on these points before moving on:

- **Stakeholders:** In recent years, we have seen an influx of different types of investors. In times past, bank managers, employees, family, and even friends were our main stakeholders. They knew you personally and had a long-term interest in your growth. Now there is actually a deeper pocket within the world of investment, but the rules here have also changed. So it is not only about finding these pockets, but it means that you must understand how to work with and attract these new investors.
- **Shareholders:** Investments have evolved, with more types of people dabbling in stock markets. However, recent and ongoing volatility in the financial markets is enough to unnerve even the most seasoned investor. These large numbers of consumers who

are purchasing stock do not have the same criteria as old-school investors, who were looking for solid long-term investment vehicles. They are interested in short-term gains. This puts enormous pressure on entrepreneurs to illustrate how they will be able to deliver these seemingly instant returns.

- **Information Access:** There is a new reporter on the block, disseminating information at a breakneck pace. Technology has opened the door for consumers to do their own research about a company's growth and potential for a return. To follow a company that they are interested in, these investors do not necessarily focus on investment books and reports but instead get their information from blogs and social networking sites like Twitter or Facebook. They view companies with a different set of parameters now, which means that you need to learn what these parameters are and then respond to them.

WHEN OBSTACLES BECOME OPPORTUNITIES

Although all these rules clearly present old and new obstacles alike, your biggest challenge may actually surprise you because it can come from such an unexpected source. In many cases— but not all—an entrepreneur's biggest obstacle can be friends and family. They can have a tendency to discourage you and attempt to dissuade you from pursuing your business ideas. Almost every entrepreneur has encountered this scenario. They are full of enthusiasm and drive to succeed with their new business and along comes a naysayer who fills them with doubt about their new venture. Again, this is not actually a bad thing; it can be an opportunity to help you refocus and refine your business idea or direction.

Along the way, it may be necessary to alter your business plan if compelling reasons for change arise. Often, when in the middle of a business or situation, your perspective can become clouded. Constructive criticism can actually serve as a map to chart a new course. Suddenly, Plan A can morph into a series of changes, all the way down to Plan C or even Plan Z.

Others' insights might seem bad if you choose to see them that way, but changing your attitude can help you see their point or see another idea based on their feedback. Either way, you can choose to give in to what is viewed as negative (not something you would do, given your status as a modern entrepreneur) or you can pick it up and run with it.

Consider the following:

- Use these comments as stones to build a stronger foundation for your business.
- Take their feedback and construct a sounding board to connect to your target audience. You must remember that very few business plans resemble their first draft.
- Harness your innate creativity to diversify and sculpt your business plan into a working model of success.
- Tackle negative feedback head-on and twist it until it becomes a benefit.

Opportunities abound, and we must take constructive criticism, regroup our ideas, and move forward with a renewed sense of purpose.

- Increased competition will impact your ability to get noticed. This is an opportunity and reason to make key changes to your strategy.
- Copycats infringe on your spotlight. Keep your ideas close and your enemies (copycats) closer. Find out what is going on in the market and use that to your advantage.
- Internet awareness can make or break you. Use it as a tool for interaction and as a two-way street strategy. Do not try to use traditional marketing ploys that tell customers what they want; let them tell you.
- Tightening regulations call for some unique solutions. This is simply a way to push you to be more creative in creating and marketing your products and services. Do not let regulations slow you down. There are always loopholes.
- Restricted resources require you to do more with much less. Real entrepreneurs thrive on and get excited by such challenges. Seeing how you can make what you have go the distance means that, in the long run, you could realize a greater profitability.
- Talent and skills gaps leave many areas of your business underperforming. Use networking to find the key talent and experts you need to help by seeking out other entrepreneurs through social networking and traditional networking practices.
- Financial limitations can complicate getting your business up and running as fast as you want or even at all. Think outside of the box by using new types of funding channels now available.

NEW RULES:
FUNDING STARTUPS

YOU ARE IN A new era of funding for startups. The rules have changed, as have the players. But one thing has remained constant: capital is critical. It is the building block that we all use to construct our businesses. An infusion of funds can stabilize your business and provide you with a solid foundation for continued growth. It is imperative to look for different sources of capital to increase your ability to fund your fledgling business and expand your operations.

What is clear is that the world has changed and all of us must embrace different strategies to succeed in today's ever-changing and ever-expanding marketplace. But you might be wondering what exactly is different and how do you go about finding the funding you need to fuel your ideas and businesses.

YESTERDAY'S GONE: WHEN VENTURE CAPITALISTS RULED

Traditionally, friends and family were a rich source of funding for a startup. It was not uncommon to tap into and secure seed money from your close friends and relatives. The relationship was mutual because they were happy to help. This was often based on a high degree of trust and enthusiasm for your business. They were banking on you as much as they were on your idea. The same could be said of informal investors. These investment sources looked to areas they were familiar with to invest their funds. For example, informal investors who were knowledgeable about tech companies would be comfortable with and would focus their capital investments toward these types of companies.

However, funding sources began to change in the 1970s. Venture capitalists came on the scene and became major players in start-up funding. A venture capitalist is a person or firm willing to provide capital for a business venture that is either starting up or wants to expand and expects to get a high rate of return for that investment. Silicon Valley and the San Francisco Bay area took on a significant role in the emergence of venture capitalists. They began to invest heavily in startups based in these areas. They had the ability to control the current management, and their power allowed them to add or change management at will if they were dissatisfied. Venture capitalists changed the playing field. No longer was it a friend or relative who was funding your business. Now startups were dealing with venture capitalists who could pull the purse strings and flex their financial muscles to maneuver and operate within a company.

TODAY'S HYBRID: A NEW FRONTIER

You may have noticed some changes in recent years. For example, there has been an emergence of a hybrid model, which combines traditional start-up financing with venture capitalism. Today's informal investor can merge with a venture capitalist to unite and fund a startup online with the creation of Internet-based companies like Kickstarter and Angel-Soft, which offer a platform for companies and individuals to request funds to develop their business or endeavor.

These new funding platforms allow people to invest in unproven, risky, or uncertain business ventures that would never be considered by traditional funding channels like banks or venture capitalists. They typically act as a way to fill the gaps in funding between what friends and family can provide and what you might be able to obtain in financing and loans from traditional sources.

In addition to handing over money, though, these so-called angel investors are interested in serving as mentors, sharing their Rolodex of contacts, making introductions for networking purposes, and providing experts who can help with certain aspects of the business. Essentially, they are interested in doing whatever it takes to transform the business venture into one that's proven, safe, and certain, as well as one that delivers an excellent return. And because they would like to achieve a high return for their high risk, angel investors often want an equity stake in the business. So that angel sitting on your shoulder may also be sitting on your board or visiting you at the office.

Angels can come from numerous places—they can be friends, family, and colleagues, but they can also be found through venture capital networks and online social networking groups and traditional networking associations. A January 1998 article by David R. Evanson and Art Beroff titled "Heaven Sent: Seeking an Angel Investor? Here's How to Find a Match Made in Heaven" in *Entrepreneur* magazine described various types of angel investor personality types:

- Corporate Angels are former executives from large companies who are now interested in taking investment money and putting it into a company where they can also turn it into a new career.
- Entrepreneurial Angels are those who already own and operate their own successful business but are looking for companies that share values or core competencies that can serve their company while helping another one to grow.
- Enthusiast Angels tend to be older, independently wealthy individuals who are investing as a hobby and may put a little bit of money into a number of companies but take a less active role in these companies.
- Micromanagement Angels want to be heavily involved in the daily operations and want control in return for their investments.
- Professional Angels are already in a profession and want to invest in a company where their expertise could be valuable to that startup or small business in terms of technology, finance, or law.

One prime example of an angel investor is Gust, which took flight when Angel-Soft rebranded and relaunched itself under this new moniker in 2011. Angel-Soft was originally formed in 2004 by David Rose as a means of providing investors with an arena to meet and collaborate with entrepreneurs and develop strategies to the mutual benefit of both parties.

With Gust, entrepreneurs can develop a comprehensive profile, assemble an investor relations outline, and work together with investors to secure funding. Investors have the ability to prescreen and filter startups based on search parameters. The word on the street has been positive, and Gust has enjoyed the endorsement of many associations.

A 2009 report by Nesta titled "Siding with the Angels," by Robert E. Wiltbank, noted that angel investing has been used widely in the United Kingdom as a financing source. The report cited that the 158 angel investors in the United Kingdom who took part in their study made 1,080 investments that totaled £134 million. Of these, 674 were still ongoing. The conclusions were that, although angel investing can be risky for the investor, it does generate some attractive returns that make these investors willing to continue searching for business ideas and entrepreneurs to bank on. Those ventures that proved successful were the ones where investors did their due diligence and stayed connected to entrepreneurs and industries they knew. As an entrepreneur then, you need to think about how you can provide these angel investors with the due diligence they seek and offer them channels in which they can participate and help you ensure a successful business.

JUST GIVE ME A PUSH: HOW KICKSTARTER PROPELLED THE CROWDFUNDING INDUSTRY

Gust is not the only online source for revenue. Many Internet-based companies are starting up and joining forces to merge financing with creative power. The power of the Internet has created this hybrid source for financing. Another company that has people standing up and taking notice is Kickstarter, which makes use of a tactic called crowdfunding.

Kickstarter jumped into action in 2009. Their role has been to cater primarily to entrepreneurs who are seeking capital for creative endeavors, ranging from films and music to writing projects and everything in between. Entrepreneurs must describe—essentially sell—their project or idea and then establish a minimum funding amount. If their fund level is not met, then all promised money is returned to the investors.

However, if the minimum is met—and, on certain projects, entrepreneurs have received much more than their intended amount—then the entrepreneur collects the promised funding.

A writer at the *New York Times* has spoken highly of this crowdfunding company, detailing how entrepreneurs were turning to Kickstarter instead of traditional avenues to establish and launch their businesses. Entrepreneurs Tom Gerhardt and Dan Provost were two people profiled in the article. Writer Steven Kurutz described their invention and why they used Kickstarter instead of pursuing alternative sources:

> Both men had degrees in environmental design and were working at design firms in Manhattan when they came up with the idea for the Glif, a plastic tripod mount and stand for the iPhone 4. They raised more than $137,000 on Kickstarter last fall, partnered with a factory in South Dakota and now sell the Glif for twenty dollars on their Web site. By April, Mr. Gerhardt and Mr. Provost, who are both twenty-seven, were successful enough to quit their day jobs and start their own design firm, Studio

Neat. That was around the time they introduced their second Kickstarter project—a stylus for the iPad they call the Cosmonaut—for which they raised about $134,000. They could have used Quirky.com, a social product development site that accepts ideas from inventors, handles the manufacturing and then pays them a royalty. But, "for us, Kickstarter was the only option," Mr. Gerhardt said. "A big thing was having control over the project."[1]

Other crowdfunding options are taking off around the world. Case in point is Symbid, a Dutch organization that is expanding to offer its financing channel to a larger expanse of the entrepreneur landscape. Members of Symbid can list an existing business or simply an idea on the Web site, along with what they would like to do, how much money they need to raise, and what the funds will be used for. In exchange, they can receive anywhere from €20,000 to a maximum of €2.5 million. For those funds, however, the entrepreneur must note how much equity they will exchange. For someone who would like to invest, they can put in as little as €20 for a stake in the business or the idea.

Symbid does make sure that the funds are used for what the entrepreneur says they will be by using separate bank accounts for the funding money so that this works for both the entrepreneur and the investor. The investor can choose to withdraw those proceeds and then invest in other potential businesses or ideas. The site uses a secure separate bank account for all investments to ensure the money is used specifically for the business idea; until the funding goal is met, investors can freely withdraw their money from one project and put it into another. Once the amount that the entrepreneur needs is met, then all the investors and the entrepreneur are tied together as part of that business so that, going forward, investors can lay claim to their stake in the new organization.

Symbid recognizes the importance of having a social networking element as part of the crowdfunding model. That's why it has an online community where entrepreneurs and investors can interact, work on their new ventures, exchange ideas and information, and generate even more businesses and opportunities.[2]

The benefits of hybrid financing cannot be overlooked. They clearly can prove to be a rich source of funding for your business while maintaining control of your vision. This shows how you should always think outside the box for new and creative ways to fund your business and redefine your boundaries.

However, that is not to say that traditional funding is dead in the water. On the contrary, traditional funding accounts for more than 90 percent of capital financing for startups. The role of establishing personal relationships and the ability to look a person in the eye has certainly not been diminished. Furthermore, it is important to emphasize that building in-depth personal relationships can still lead to the development of key financing sources or investor relationships that can help you start up or expand your business.

This is because investors tend to invest in people as much as they invest in ideas. They want to see presentations and watch management up close to see how they operate and interact within a particular setting. This is because they want to be a part of something that succeeds, knowing that their financial support helped to create that success. Investors tend to base 80 percent of their decisions on the quality of the management and their feel of a person based on personal interaction. You cannot replace this traditional funding model. Investors are human and they want to make a connection to size up a situation and person.

THE GOVERNMENT CONNECTION: SMALL BUSINESS ADMINISTRATION LOANS

Other sources should also be considered, including a government connection. At E Factor, we are strong believers in researching the Small Business Administration (SBA) for seed money to develop or expand your business.

Historically, seed money is the most difficult to secure. Most traditional investors only want to invest in companies that show a positive cash flow statement, unless you are dealing with friends and family, who might be willing to assume more risks. One alternative, therefore, is an SBA loan, which makes it possible to secure funds to reach your goals. Their Web site (www.sba.gov) provides detailed information for entrepreneurs to research and apply for loans that meet their needs.

EVERYBODY GET IN LINE: THE ROAD TO REVENUE

As you can see here, there are actually many sources of financing for your startup or expansion of your existing business. To realize your funding and investment goals, look to these steps before you proceed:

1. Look to an SBA-guaranteed loan for seed money if you are in the United States. Similar government-based financing programs are available in most countries. This will allow you to demonstrate that you have the ability to launch and maintain a business.

2. Next, secure financing as your business develops, which can include asking friends and family about additional funds for your business.

3. Scout out informal investors who have experience in your field and are interested in investing in a new venture through networking and social networking.

4. Consider crowdfunding as one of the top alternative funding methods now available. It can help you reach your goal quickly thanks to many supporters.

5. Once you are established and show a positive revenue statement, discuss your options with a venture capitalist. The days of simply having a business plan and finding venture capitalists to fund it fully are over. You must prove you have the savvy to succeed before they will consider investing with you.

Using these steps demonstrates how you can go from one to four as listed above quite easily. You can build your business plan and gauge the point at which your business is operating.

IS IT JUST ME OR IS IT CROWDED IN HERE?

Although there are many sources for funding, even more people want to get their hands on that money. It has become a crowded marketplace where businesses are all competing for the same small pool of resources to fund their latest ventures. Competition increases daily, and you must outmaneuver them, wrestle control, and win the prize. And of course, the prize is in the form of capital.

Let us look at some different potential challenges you may need to be familiar with as you go through Steps 1 to 5:

- **Your Local Bank:** The option of securing a loan from your local bank to fund your startup is almost non-existent today. You need major capital and assets to secure a bank loan, which makes this option essentially unusable for most people. They demand you open your life and pledge all your assets to secure a bank loan. Until market conditions improve, banks are a poor source for funding.

- **Know Your Own Worth:** There are endless accounts of entrepreneurs who get into trouble by not knowing their own worth. They lack the confidence in themselves and their business to ask for the correct amount of money up front. They fear investors will be scared off if they ask for too much money. But what ends up happening is they ask for half of a million dollars when they actually need millions. Then they have to come back again in a short amount of time to raise additional funding. In the end, the only thing that they accomplish is a loss of credibility with those they borrowed from, so it is important to have a precise figure that will account for all your operational and start-up needs. So know your own worth and do not be afraid to ask for the money you will need to succeed. It will showcase your professionalism and knowledge.

- **Friends and Family Still Count:** Despite often being viewed as an outdated source, friends and family are still excellent sources for any entrepreneur looking to get started. One of the best stories to relate is that of the famed San Francisco restaurant chain The

Slanted Door, founded by Charles Phan. He has built one of the city's most loved restaurants thanks to help from his family and their total of twenty credit cards. His family believed in his abilities as a chef, business owner, and hard worker. This encapsulates why family and friends are the best channels. Unlike complete strangers such as those associated with a venture capital firm or an angel investor, your friends and family believe in you and your ideas. They have most likely known you all their lives. This becomes more of an emotional investment than one solely grounded in Return on Investment (ROI). Then, it is up to you to show through your actions that their belief in you was the right choice.

- **Some Other Avenues to Consider:** In looking for protection and security when securing financing, you might want to consider a Private Placement Memorandum (PPM) as this provides a detailed outline of potential risks to the investor. A private placement is considered a non-public offering in contrast with an initial public offering, which companies use to raise funds to grow their business. Private placement is a way to raise funds through a small, select group of private investors. When used within the United States, these must be registered with the Securities and Exchange Commission (SEC) to make sure they follow all the stipulations found under the Securities Act of 1933. Once the funds are raised, they are usually in the form of stocks, warrants, promissory notes, shares of common or preferred stock, or some other kind of membership. These are then purchased by institutional investors like a bank, a pension fund, or an insurance company. One advantage of a PPM is that it can protect you from fraud complaints and it can serve as a sales tool to investors. If you do decide to use a PPM, be sure to have an attorney draw it up for you to make sure it complies with the letter of the law.

Sponsors are another option. This is a great way to help fund your business because sponsors will pay money in return for exposure. Many business owners are willing to do this because they are looking for an effective way to stimulate their own businesses and gain publicity without having to use a lot of resources (time and money) to do so. This was one of the funding avenues we used in getting E Factor off the ground. To this day, we still use sponsorship money as a way to help grow our business and we suggest you think about doing the same.

Sponsorship can involve receiving funds, but it can also mean some type of in-kind resource or barter deal that can be just as valuable to your business. The sponsorship opportunity can be varied and you can offer your sponsors short-term or long-term publicity, depending on the size of the funding or in-kind resource they provide. The business-to-business sponsorships tend to involve a longer working relationship and lead to other opportunities, such as co-branding, for the benefit of both firms. The important aspect to remember when turning to sponsorships is to create a mutually beneficial situation for you and your sponsor so that they can see a return on their investment and continue to provide resources for you. However, if you choose to use more than one sponsor, make sure that every party is amenable to the situation so that one sponsor does not feel another one is getting priority. It is about balance and communication in order to maintain what can be a very beneficial funding channel over the long term.

E FACTOR FINANCE REQUEST

One of the leading tools on E Factor's site is the Finance Request tool. The Finance Request allows E Factor members to get in touch with potential investors in order to take their business plan to the next step. The process is very easy and straight-forward; E Factor members simply fill out a six-step question-naire that asks basic questions about their prospective business venture. The questionnaire has members give brief descriptions of their role in the company, the business plan, and the infor-mation on the products and services the business will provide. Members are then asked to name the amount of investment money they are looking for and what type of investment.

Once the questionnaire is filled out, the Finance Request pro-posal is reviewed by E Factor for approval. Approved requests are then posted to the member's profile page for investors to review. Investors who match what the member is looking for will be notified. All investors, however, are able to view the proposal. If an investor is interested in a member's Finance Request, then the member and investor can get into contact for further communication and discussion through E Factor mail.

DRIMPY USES E FACTOR'S FINANCE REQUEST

Drimpy is an online social networking site that allows patients, caregivers, and healthcare professionals to exchange dialogue via the Internet. The site creates a platform for patients to seek advice from other patients and caregivers and receive more immediate answers to their health-related questions from their doctor. Patients are able to get dependable advice and information through this social network of fellow patients, caregivers, and doctors before, during, and after treatment. This type of "participatory health" or "social health" is optimal for patients because they have access to a number of different sources of information. These multiple outlets allow patients to have more personal control over their own health and, ultimately, their quality of life. A variety of sources also enable patients to "manage, control, and improve the treatment and healing process in cooperation with all healthcare organizations involved." Because Drimpy operates as an independent body, completely separate from the healthcare institutions themselves, it can provide unbiased and genuine information to patients.

When founder and CEO Arnold Breukhoven combined his two passions, business and medicine, to create Drimpy, he realized how helpful E Factor's tools really can be. In an interview, Breukhoven said that he has been an E Factor member since the site's launch in the Netherlands. He said he was planning on using personal funds; he also had a few investors from previous existing business connections. Breukhoven said that E Factor co-founder Marion Freijsen was the one who suggested that he fill out a Finance Request. He said that Marion has acted as his business mentor since he joined E Factor. Her suggestions were valuable to him and he decided to fill out the questionnaire. Breukhoven also noted that his Finance Request form received interest almost immediately—within a week of filling it out. Once investors expressed interest in Drimpy, Arnold was able to contact them directly to secure investments.

LESSONS LEARNED

Throughout the interview, Breukhoven continued to stress how valuable his interactions with E Factor have been. First and foremost, he mentioned the mentorship that Marion, along with the counsel of other E Factor members and board members, had provided him. Breukhoven also gives a lot of credit to the events E Factor hosts, which allow face-to-face contact with business professionals and allow E Factor members to build their networks in person. It takes the virtual aspect of E Factor and makes it much more concrete and physical.

When asked what advice or tips he would give to E Factor members, Breukhoven responded enthusiastically by saying, "Do it!" He says that there is nothing to lose by putting an inquiry out there, especially because the Finance Request is so simple to complete. In this instance, the potential for positive return vastly outweighs the negatives. The worst possible outcome is that you will not find an investor, in which case you are back to where you started. In reference to the work ethic required to get a company off the ground, Breukhoven noted, "You have to take everything you can find and do everything possible to make it happen." He also said, "You don't care how much time it takes!" Fortunately, completing the Finance Request form is not time-consuming, making the E Factor tool that much more advantageous for entrepreneurs.

YOUR PLAN OF ACTION

Developing strategies for securing financing becomes easier when you know where to look. Be diligent and prepared. Focus

your resources and refine your technique because the success of
your business depends on you—how you approach your funding collection and how you manage those funds once you have
them.

KEY POINTS TO REMEMBER

- Your friends and family, as well as personal contacts,
  are still some of the best funding sources. They support you unconditionally and believe in your dream
  nearly as much as you do.
- Crowdfunding and group lending are new channels
  to consider. These work especially well for smaller
  business ideas that simply need a jolt of capital to get
  them going.
- Traditional small-business loans and grants are still
  available. You just need to spend more time and
  make the right contacts to connect with those who
  can help you.
- Ask and you shall receive. Take advantage of online
  networking and traditional networking channels in
  order to connect with those who can provide funding, as well as other vital skills to ensure the money
  received produces the necessary results. This means
  working with angel investors and venture capitalists
  who can provide resources and mentoring, as well
  as connections to talent and advisors to stimulate
  the potential of your startup or grow your existing
  business.

NEW TOOLS OF ENGAGEMENT: THE WORLD OF SOCIAL MEDIA

A REVOLUTION IS IN progress as tools like Facebook, Twitter, YouTube, blogs, microblogs, and Web sites, which most of us use regularly—if not every day—evolve to create new social media opportunities for entrepreneurs. We can harness these social media and social networking tools to inform, engage, and entice our customers. We can develop these applications and use them to promote our businesses and realize our full potential.

However, with social media and social networking, the terms have a tendency to become interchangeable. But each is a distinct and separate entity that can be tailored to build your brand, increase your marketing profile, develop strong brand recognition, nurture new product development, and increase your funding options.

In the following sections we will define social media and social networking, as well as discuss the business strategies and tools we can employ to use each application to develop our brand and business fully.

SOCIAL MEDIA VS. SOCIAL NETWORKING: AS DIFFERENT AS NIGHT AND DAY

Many people use the terms *social media* and *social networking* interchangeably. However, each application has a unique identity and function. As we move through explaining social media and social networking, we will see how each one plays an important role in influencing and molding your business.

- **Social Media:** Social media is a tool used to transmit information to a wide audience. Social media imparts a message to a consumer and delivers this information via the Internet. You are the storyteller and your customer is your audience.
- **Social Networking:** Social networking engages your customer and develops a relationship with them. Connections are made with groups or individuals who share a common thread or interest. There is a give and take with social networking in which you are engaged with the consumer. Conversation is the key, and the customer becomes your partner.

Knowing how to stimulate conversation among your followers and position your communication to deliver a strong and clear message will provide you with a powerful one-two punch to increase your business and position your company.

Facebook: The Choice of a New Generation of Consumers

Facebook is a social networking site that has become an industry leader with more than eight hundred million active users. Its genius is its simple premise in that it allows users to communicate with friends and companies. This allows for a free flow of information between both parties. Your job as an entrepreneur is to connect Facebook to your mass-marketing campaign and cultivate endorsements for new product developments and existing brands. That's what Facebook is all about for businesses—a mass-marketing tool for entrepreneurs who seize the opportunity to position their retail strategy for success.

Connecting a mass-marketing campaign with Facebook followers can increase your business presence and develop additional revenue sources through connections. You can add an update and encourage conversation with status reports and sales information.

Twitter: Getting the Conversation Started

While Facebook is social networking, Twitter is social media. Period. With Twitter, we broadcast short blasts of information to our followers. They can respond back, but only with 140 characters at a time. This doesn't make for meaningful conversation, but it does position you and your company for microblogging that delivers a dominant message to your subscribers. You can continually feed your followers information about a new product, remind them of a launch date, or advertise a sale, all with the "sound bites" Twitter provides.

According to Twitter, 200 million users tweet in real time to reach an audience. An entrepreneur can use Twitter as a tool to target a specific group with a particular message. Microblogging can increase your company profile and name recognition within a certain target audience.

YouTube: Adding Visuals to Your Social Networking Repertoire

YouTube is a video-sharing Web site created in 2005 by three former PayPal employees. YouTube made it possible for ordinary users to upload and share videos easily via the Internet.

YouTube works as a vehicle of social media that merges into social networking to create connections among interested viewers. Entrepreneurs can use YouTube's unique position as both a social media outlet and a social networking route to promote a product or cause to a specific target audience.

YouTube also makes it possible for a video to "go viral," which offers entrepreneurs a variety of advantages. However, consider this scenario: You have created a funny video promoting your product. People love it! They begin sharing it with friends and the next thing you know, your video has gone viral and is being aired on the seven o'clock news. You pat yourself on the back, tell yourself how wonderful you are, and begin wondering how many additional units you will sell. But just remember, the powers that be can take it away just as quickly as they give it. Say your product falls flat on its face and is considered a disaster. People will be only too happy to upload a video to YouTube to point this out.

LinkedIn: Making the Professional Network Connection

LinkedIn is a professional social media site where members can create a profile describing their businesses, education, and accomplishments. After you make connections, you can network and find additional contacts you can use to your advantage.

One effective tool LinkedIn offers is the ability to view your associates' contacts. This can prove useful if you are trying to gain an introduction. Say you are interested in connecting with the CEO of Company A. You browse an associate's connections and you see that they are linked to this particular CEO. You can use this information to request an introduction. This makes LinkedIn a powerful social media site. E Factor, the world's largest community of entrepreneurs, has its own social networking function. You can read more about how E Factor's social networking community works in Chapter 5.

Google+: Adding to the Social Channels

Google+ was introduced on a limited invitation-only basis in 2011. Within four weeks of its debut, it had reached twenty-five million visitors. Dubbed a social networking site, Google+ offers a variety of features:

- **Circles.**
  - This feature allows users to interface and make contact with groups for sharing.
- **Messenger.**
  - This lets users share photos and instant messages via Android, iPhone, and SMS devices.

- **Hangouts.**
  - ○ This refers to a group video link, which can now be hooked up with YouTube to suggest videos to other users.

Google+ is still relatively new and its full business capabilities and limitations are still to be seen and proven.

Blogs and Web sites: Still Relevant as the Credibility Builders

Blogs have been used successfully on corporate Web sites to introduce new products, inform clients of upcoming innovations, and notify consumers of upcoming sales and specials. Blogs have also proven to be valuable social media outlets with informative topics that appeal to a broad range of customers. You are not merely going for a sale but giving potential customers additional information so they can make an informed purchase. Customers appreciate this and blogs offer a way to shape and mold your business's public perception. You can use your blog as a public relations vehicle by being helpful, concerned, and engaged with your customers' concerns.

Corporate Web sites are still a main social media platform. Your company's identity and brand begin here. Viewers can research your Web site to get a general feel of your company's identity. Never underestimate the power of branding. Your logo, colors, and content should be universal.

Case Study on Social Media—Fashion Retail's Social Media Hits and Misses as Told by Missoni and Target

High-fashion collaborations with Target Corporation, one of the nation's biggest discount retail chains, are not a new phenomenon. Starting in 2007 with the Proenza Schouler GO International series, Target has partnered with a long list of top-tier designers. Their latest project with Missoni, an Italian fashion house founded in 1953, was launched on September 13, 2011. Although Target did not publish an official press release on the partnership until August 15, 2011, news of the collection was announced via the @TargetStyle Twitter account on May 4, 2011, and on Vogue.com. The news was picked up by multiple online sources as well. The hype produced by Target's PR team created an extraordinary amount of buzz among the online community of fashion enthusiasts. On the morning of the collection's release, customers were lined up outside Target stores nationwide in order to get their hands on low-priced Missoni items.

The customer response was everything Target had hoped for—and more—maybe even too much. Stores were ransacked, customers were fighting each other over throw pillows, and the Target.com Web site crashed. Orders placed online did not go through, online customers were charged the wrong prices, and orders were never delivered. Customers were furious and many claimed that they would never shop at Target again. How did Target use social media to create such an avid customer group? Did Target employ the power of social media to overcome the damage to their reputation? Let's find out about their social media hits and misses.

GENERATING HYPE: TWITTER

The Missoni for Target PR campaign took full advantage of social media outlets. Multiple Twitter accounts all highlighted the approaching clothing launch: @Target, @TargetStyle, @Missoni, and @MargheritaMissoni featured regular tweets, touting the upcoming affordable designer collaboration. The

Twitter account responsible for clothing- and fashion-related posts, @TargetStyle, provided a more fashion-friendly platform for both relevant Target products and fashion-focused customers. This element of the social media campaign was necessary to appeal to current Target clothing customers. On the morning of the Missoni collaboration announcement, more than one hundred Twitter followers retweeted the exciting news.

Margherita's role in the social media campaign was critical to involve the fashion conscious. As a fashion icon, she bolstered credibility for the low-priced collection because of her obvious connection with the Missoni name. Her style-icon status put her at an advantage because her fashion choices are so trusted. She was active on her Twitter account, tweeting about the line and retweeting Missoni for Target–related tweets from Target Twitter accounts and excited customers. The use of Margherita's Twitter account created buzz among elite designer customers. It was also a good move in order to transform Missoni fans into Missoni for Target fans, pulling in customers who might not necessarily shop at Target.

GENERATING HYPE: THE MARINA DOLL BLOG

One of the more ingenious ploys introduced by the Target PR team was the creation of Marina and her Tumblr blog, *All the Way Up Here*. As defined by Tumblr, this is a microblogging site that lets you share text, photos, quotes, links, music, and videos from your browser, phone, desktop, or e-mail that is completely customizable. The entries were written from the perspective of a doll named Marina. The premise was "Marina's absolutely must-read, incredibly fashionable style blog." The sidebar had an icon that read "I love these guys! Target & Missoni. I can't believe I'm working for them and they're sending me to New

York Fashion Week! So Cool!" The Tumblr was created in early April and had posts about Marina's travels in Italy, her idolization of Missoni, and her stay in Varese, the town where Missoni originated. Marina then conducted snail mail correspondence with Margherita Missoni and Twitter conversations. The blog also highlighted the different products in the Missoni for Target line, such as the beach cruiser bicycle, and announced different Twitter-based competitions.

The Marina doll blog represents the complementary nature of social media outlets. The blog introduced an advocate of the Missoni brand, the Missoni for Target collection, and current style trends. Given that Marina's blog posts had a variety of topics and did not necessarily all contain direct mentions of Missoni, her blog was able to develop into a source of style and lifestyle advice, while praising Missoni ingenuity at the same time. Marina also had a Twitter account that had more than a thousand followers who interacted with her about the Missoni launch and made various style comments. The symbiotic relationship between Marina's Twitter account and her blog is a good example of the way Twitter and a blog can be used together in a promotion. Marina's blog made references to Twitter while at the same time her Twitter posts announced new blog posts. Marina's Twitter and blog also interacted with other aspects of Target's marketing campaign by retweeting @TargetStyle Tweets, interacting with Margherita Missoni's Twitter posts, and providing information about the product launch. The Twitter hashtag #MissoniforTarget was also trending on Twitter. Although this was not an element of the social media campaign that Target introduced, it can be considered a positive representation of all the work the Target PR team had done for the product launch.

GENERATING HYPE: FACEBOOK

No specific Facebook accounts were created for Missoni for Target. Instead, Target used its already established TargetStyle Facebook page to deliver news about the Missoni collaboration. The Target Facebook page was also used for announcements and updates on the product launch. It should be noted, however, that it did not announce the initial news of the collaboration. This omission shows how Target tried to focus the social media attention on fashion-related platforms. Although the Target Facebook page did give a few mentions of the Missoni line, such as the release of the "look book," the TargetStyle Facebook page carried most of the weight.

The TargetStyle Facebook page gave Facebook users small Missoni for Target sneak peeks in the months following the announcement: pictures of the Missoni for Target clothing tag, reminders of the upcoming collection, and recurring posts asking Facebook users what their favorite piece of the collection was. This last element is a perfect example of the way social media platforms should be used—to get participants interacting with the page. These Facebook posts generated a lot of interactions. The question "If you had to pick just one (we know it's difficult), what's your favorite Missoni for Target item?" generated 128 likes and 64 comments. Posts relating the number of days until the release of the collection were also highly effective in generating contact between Facebook users and the Facebook page, with 379 likes on the ten-day countdown post.

GENERATING HYPE: OTHER MARKETING PROJECTS

Other projects that Target's marketing team worked on were the Missoni for Target television ads and print ads in *Vogue* magazine, in which there were multipage spreads in both the August and September issues. The New York Fashion Week Missoni for Target Pop-Up Shop also generated a lot of buzz among fans of the collection. The Pop-Up Shop was supposed to stay open for three days and offer customers a chance to buy the low-priced Missoni collaboration four days before the launch. A photo was posted on the Target Facebook page of the Missoni for Target Pop-Up Shop and it received more than a thousand likes. The Marina Doll was brought to the Pop-Up Shop location and updates on the event were posted across all social media platforms.

THE SOCIAL MEDIA FAUX PAS

All of these elements employed by the Target marketing team were very successful—so much so that it created an unprecedented amount of demand for a very limited amount of product. Eager customers lined up outside of Target stores nationwide well before the opening hour to ensure that they had the first pick of Missoni goods. In-store customers said they fought with other Missoni for Target buyers over clothing and some even saw people stealing items out of other customers' carts. Customers also flooded Target.com, reporting that they kept watch on the site in order to be the first ones to order merchandise. They had been under the impression that the collection would go on sale at 12:00 A.M. on September 13.

Instead, many disappointed customers had to wait until the collection went up for sale at 8:00 A.M. The rush of activity kept the site from running, and the whole site eventually crashed. The Web site crash caused online orders to stop mid-process, with some customers unable to complete their transactions. Other customers received confirmation of their orders but either got the wrong items or had very delayed delivery. Overall, customers were not pleased with the chaos and stress that surrounded the launch of the Missoni for Target collection.

THE RESPONSE—MISSING THE SOCIAL MEDIA MARK

On September 16, three days after the collection's launch, Target issued a press release regarding the Missoni for Target orders made on Target.com. The three-sentence statement simply said that the unprecedented demand created high levels of traffic on the Web site, which ultimately affected the delivery of orders.

The statement also mentioned Target's commitment to customer service and that they would "have a team dedicated to addressing those guests who have been affected." Target's response to the situation, although straightforward, appeared to be very unsympathetic. Customers were frustrated by the fact that while in the midst of entering payment information onto a Web site it froze without any explanation of what would happen to the order. Even after the event had passed, Target still seemed unable to provide specific answers. That's a huge mistake when it comes to leveraging social media.

WHEN SOCIAL MEDIA BITES BACK

The social media and networking platforms that had been so busy in the time before the Missoni for Target launch continued to show many interactions. This time, however, fans of the collection were not so pleased. Negative comments poured over all of Target's social media sites and anti-Target social media outlets started appearing. The hashtag #targetfail and the Twitter account @BoycottTarget are two examples of the massive public outrage.

Comments on the Target and TargetStyle Facebook pages related customers' frustrations: "Target: the fact that you didn't anticipate the online demand after the almost excessive media attention this collection received means there was very poor planning. The site crashing is totally ridiculous." Other comments included, "Seriously, what's wrong with this Web site? SO FRUSTRATED AT TARGET!!" and "Pathetic. And a horrible marketing move."

DAMAGE CONTROL

Although Target was effectively active with their social media use in the months, days, and hours leading up to the launch of Missoni for Target, it seemed that they disappeared from the scene in the wake of a marketing event gone horribly wrong. Before 8:00 A.M. on the day of the launch, the TargetStyle Facebook page already had angry comments on how the Web site wasn't working. Then, the TargetStyle Facebook account posted comments encouraging customers to be patient and to keep trying the online store. Statements like "Target.com appears to be having some issues right now. We have reached out to the appropriate teams and they're working to address the issues" and "Thank you for commenting and sharing your stories. The unprecedented demand for the Missoni for Target collection impacted our Target.com site and some guest orders. We are working hard to address affected orders and will share updates as they become available" were posted on the TargetStyle Facebook page. At this point, the Target customers who were posting angry comments on Facebook were very upset and there wasn't a real acknowledgment of their frustrations. Customers were just told to continue to be patient and keep checking back.

Comments on the quickly sold-out merchandise in stores were largely found on various Twitter accounts. Tweets regarding the mayhem that had ensued the morning of the launch could easily be found with the #missonifortarget and #targetfail hashtags. The TargetStyle and Target Twitter accounts did a better job of individually addressing upset customers. The same tone of response, however, continued. Many fans inquiring over the possibility of more merchandise were simply answered with Tweets like "@ErinFoltz to our knowledge, we will not be restocking." Other responses directed customers to a customer relations phone line. Again, the facts were simply stated and customers were not given the emotional satisfaction of remorse. This tone gave the impression that Target did not have control over the outcome, even though it is agreed by many resources that they could have done things differently to control the crowds and buying frenzy.

In reviewing the responses by various social media outlets, Target never apologized for the situation but instead gave the impression that they could not do anything. In fact, Target's response to the situation at first offered some semblance of hope by suggesting that customers continue to try to buy merchandise. When merchandise was finally sold-out, Target was neither apologetic nor sympathetic.

LESSONS LEARNED

If one thing can be agreed on, it is that Target did an excellent and thorough job of using social media to generate hype for the Missoni for Target collection. In the same way that Target got fans and potential customers interacting with the various social media platforms before the launch, they could have done the same to handle the negative situation that occurred after the launch. Customers who felt strongly enough about the in-store chaos or the online debacle to tweet or comment on Facebook about it should have been given more of a response. These same people were interacting with all the content Target was putting out about the collection in the days before the launch; there was no reason why Target couldn't have done the same in return. However, all of their responses felt highly impersonal and unsympathetic.

The issue here is that these Target customers turned to social media for sympathy in the first place. Posting a Facebook status about the frustration they experienced with Target.com was done in order to commiserate with others who were affected or simply to get a response that would validate their frustration. In a time when customers' views of a product or company are so easily accessible, so is information on how the company dealt with a poor interaction. The impersonal and somewhat cold response from Target will long reverberate throughout the online community.

This case study about Target and the other information in this chapter show that you must be open and versatile when approaching your social media strategies. You must be constantly aware of different avenues to pursue to realize your business's full potential. Just because something worked today does not mean it will work tomorrow or the next day. It can turn on a dime. Your success depends on a full understanding of today's ever-evolving social media outlets. It is also based on your ability to gauge and anticipate trends before they occur. This is especially true with social media and social networking. Your understanding and savvy when dealing with social media and social networking will increase sales, engage your customers, and fully benefit your business. Be a pioneer. Social media and social networking are still in their infancy. The trick is to control the flow of information and utilize these two applications to their maximum potential.

Many small companies and entrepreneurs have gotten social media right and offer more than a few ways to show up big companies and retailers on how to get the most from this new channel.

Case Study—Doing It Right with Rave Reviews: Paranormal Activity *Was Ready for Its Social Media Close-up*

The first installment of the *Paranormal Activity* movie series was released in theaters in 2007. For the release of the third installment in 2011, the entrepreneurs and minds behind the movie had very little money for marketing, but they were rich in ideas on how to scare up success with a grassroots viral marketing campaign, using social media as its script. Although the original installment was made on a direct-to-DVD budget of $11,000, the result was to create one of the most profitable movies in the history of Paramount Studios. In the United States alone, it made $108 million.

The buzz began with staging free midnight showings in select college towns where the marketers could target their audience and make the most impact. They knew that it would be advantageous to court tech-savvy college students who were most likely using Facebook and Twitter. Consequently, the word of mouth about the movie spread quickly and stimulated buzz about what appeared to be a truly scary movie experience. There were a number of channels used, including a viral Web site (www.paranormalmovie.com), a YouTube trailer that reached 16.7 million views, a Facebook fan page with nearly 670,000 fans, and a Twitter "Tweet Your Scream" campaign.

The viral social media campaign placed the success of the movie in the hands of viewers and, by doing so, ensured success. Strategies included inciting audience members to vote for *Paranormal Activity* to play in their town. In addition, positive word of mouth was fueled by "chatter" on Twitter, YouTube, and Facebook that helped spread the message in a manner rarely seen by even the highest-budget star vehicles.

LESSONS LEARNED

As an entrepreneur, money is not everything; what you need is creativity and the drive to market in new ways. You do not need to have a multinational corporation-size marketing budget or use traditional marketing methods like television and magazines. They do not necessarily work anyway. It helps to ask your audience to get involved and become part of the campaign. Often, whether it is movies or other products, consumers are now more than happy to be part of the publicity process, which draws them closer to products and brands on an emotional level.

IN THEIR OWN WORDS AND ACCORDING TO
THE MEDIA

According to Josh Greenstein, co-president of marketing for Paramount, "It was very important that we sold this as an experience rather than just a movie. When people saw the movie, they loved it so much and there is such a slow build of terror that you have to sit through to experience the full effect of the movie, so we changed the marketing techniques in advertising and online to make it more experiential. We wanted to use an experiential sell to help dictate how and where it rolled out to the consumer."

His colleague, Amy Powell, senior vice president of interactive marketing for Paramount, agreed: "We have the advantage with all these digital tools of allowing word of mouth to spread much faster than before. Winning over your fans and letting them feel included in the process is instrumental in the marketing of any film, it's just a matter of how far you take that notion. The notion of virtually shaking hands with each and every one of your fans is an incredibly intimidating one. For a long time, movie marketing was a mass-market approach that wasn't personalized—there was no thank you. For a long time Twitter was just a buzzword for more-traditional marketers, but I think this film articulated in a tangible way the importance of how big that audience could be and how vocal they can be when you embrace them as your allies."

Even the media had their take on it. Lisa Respers France of CNN noted, "Using a campaign of limited showings, social media and word-of-mouth fan buzz, the film has managed to become a breakout hit without the aid of a glitzy marketing campaign—or even a traditional movie trailer." Bill Briggs of MSNBC.com stated, "The reason [for the movie's success] is as simple as a neighborly chat. People trust their friends' film reviews—and their online friends' opinions—more than they do slick movie advertising. Of course, that shift can work to the advantage of the studios—especially those, like Paramount—that already are attracting audiences through social media pipelines. Simply put, Facebook and Twitter offer cheap advertising." Likening the movie's marketing ploys to a pioneer in viral marketing, those behind the *Blair Witch Project*, Andrew Hampp of *Advertising Age Magazine Online* said, "All the online buzz and viral marketing surrounding *Paranormal Activity* resembles the path first paved by *Blair Witch* ten years ago, but with one notable difference—credibility. At no point has Paramount pretended that the camcorder footage in *Paranormal* is anything but fiction. Paramount seems to be skewing more toward audiences' reaction to the movie itself rather than tacking a deceptive 'based on true events' tagline onto the marketing materials."[3]

Case Study—BlendTec Mixes the Right Blend of Social Media Ingredients

Imagine achieving six million views on YouTube within five days, gaining 60,000 subscribers, achieving celebrity status, and generating an estimated 500 percent increase in sales growth. That's what a small appliances company was able to achieve, and they did it thanks to a creative and fun social media strategy that cost them nearly nothing.

BlendTec was created by Tom Dickson, who has been an innovator and engineer his entire life and who has sought to make products that are unique and practical. The company now has a team of engineers who have conceptualized, manufactured, and marketed unique products that are now used in restaurants, coffee and smoothie shops, and homes all over the world. As a small company, they had an even smaller marketing budget, so they had to put that same ingenuity to work to garner attention in their marketplace. Tom Dickson noted that the idea for this social media campaign came from their objective to enhance brand awareness and showcase their products' competitive features, such as their durability, but to do so in a less obvious, funnier, and therefore memorable way.

The result was a low-budget viral video campaign that started out in 2006. A team of people from the company decided that it would be fun to create silly videos to see what could be blended in their product. They ended up on the first of what would be five videos, starring the head of the company decked out in laboratory gear. In a white lab coat and safety glasses, the CEO then proceeded to blend some rather strange ingredients, including marbles, a garden rake, McDonald's Extra Value Meals, and a rotisserie chicken. Although the budget has never been revealed, those looking at the videos believe that the ingredients and homemade video production could not have cost more than $100 per video. The videos were put out on a special Web site they created, as well as posted to YouTube and Facebook. Thousands of inbound links only further increased the viral power of their campaign as the videos were passed around. It was not long before BlendTec was getting requests about what viewers would like to see next in the blender.

The remains of an iPhone and iPod that were blended in a video went up for sale on eBay—that's how involved the viewers were. The marketing campaign worked because it was folksy and authentic. This had a lot to do with the CEO taking a starring role and in his ability to connect with his audience through his own enthusiasm and passion. People seeing the video could connect with his childish delight at the prospect of blending up different items. This made people want to tune in to see what else the company could try to blend in their experimental videos, but they made them in such a way as to balance the shock value with humor. The blending of different products also created an ingenious cross-marketing platform so that if someone was searching for "iPhone," the BlendTec videos would come up in the search results. This attracted more attention and accelerated the viral nature of what the company was doing.

In this way, BlendTec was able to turn a small household appliance into a powerful and attractive consumer product that illustrated how it was different than others within its product niche. The social media marketing strategy was so popular that the competition tried to copy the campaign, but this strategy only irritated consumers, who felt that the competition should have come up with something unique like BlendTec did rather than copying it. In this way, it only furthered the idea that BlendTec was different, thereby backfiring on the competition.

You might think that, in this fickle world, such a social media campaign would get old and boring. It has run for six years and continues to attract new and return viewers as people do not seem to grow tired of watching the company blend up all types of items. This long run has also allowed the company not only to increase their product revenue, but they are making money from the videos, thanks to ads that play at the end of the video. It turns out that other companies that recognized the audience BlendTec was attracting knew that their ads would get in front of this very large audience.

LESSONS LEARNED

Looking at what BlendTec, a small entrepreneurial company, has been able to achieve in terms of its marketing and profitability objectives illustrates how social media marketing does not have to have a large budget in order to achieve the intended results. If anything, as other examples have illustrated, a big budget may actually get in the way of real creativity—what actually makes the entrepreneur tick.

Other lessons are that content can be beneficial and lend credence to marketing efforts, but the visual nature of an online marketing strategy carries more weight and memory with a target audience, thereby further reinforcing or ingraining brand identity. Even better is to incorporate an SEO strategy within social media campaigns with product placements to build search engine visibility. Therefore, it is important to optimize with keywords and use Google AdWords within your social media advertising and marketing. You can use humor in an authentic and memorable way while balancing shock value or silliness in a way that can be engaging and help to connect with your audience. In this way, you can get your messages about your product, company, and brand across without being completely obvious. In the case of BlendTec, they were able to communicate that they and their products were dependable, innovative, durable, and high quality.

KEY POINTS TO REMEMBER

- Social media is a tool used to transmit information to a widespread audience. Social media imparts a message to a consumer and delivers this information via the Internet. You are the storyteller and your customer is your audience.

- Social networking engages your customers and develops a relationship with them. Connections are made with groups or individuals who share a common thread or interest. There is a give and take with social networking where you are engaged with the consumer. Conversation is the key, and the consumer becomes your partner.

- Numerous companies have thrived on using social media and social networking as a publicity tool and as a way to interact with their customers and potential customers. They have been able to minimize their marketing budgets while maximizing the attention and admiration they receive. Aligning offline and online strategies is even more powerful.

- Some companies can make a misstep in their rush to use social media and social networking by assuming they can use it in the same way as traditional channels. Although Target initially had success with it and was well on its way with its Missoni partnership, it worked too well and the reactions and way it was handled after the fact illustrated how quickly these tools can go wrong if not used appropriately.

NEW CONNECTIONS:
VIRTUAL NETWORKING

ALTHOUGH TRADITIONAL NETWORKING HAS always been a priority for successful entrepreneurs, the ability to reach out to investors, talent, colleagues, experts, and other stakeholders has increased exponentially thanks to the development of a virtual networking landscape of social networking. This chapter offers insights into the benefits you can leverage from virtual networking, as well as some words of caution and recommendations on how to get the most traction from it in terms of building a business and a brand.

Let's start with some of the basics on this invaluable tool. Although you may be already using some of the most well-known social networking sites—Facebook, Twitter, LinkedIn, and Google+—others who are just venturing into virtual networking may not realize just how easy it is to connect with business associates and develop relationships that will further business goals and strategies. Beyond what a physical networking event might do, the virtual world of social networking allows you to connect with people and potential clients whom you might not otherwise meet. Stop and think about whom you talk to on a regular basis. If you are an entrepreneur, you are most likely interacting with people in other states, not to mention those farther afield in other countries. That is really powerful and something that was unheard of less than a decade ago.

The opportunities that this new medium affords serve to fuel your business and career as well as provide a platform for continued growth. Social networking sites understand the need to segment and define categories and channels that enable people to identify whom they are looking for to build their contact list and networking map quickly and effectively. You might even say that virtual networking can serve as a business directory. Say you are looking for key personnel within a company. You know their function, but you might not know their name. Sites like E Factor (see the case study in this chapter), LinkedIn, and Facebook have eliminated the need to search endlessly for these business contacts. You can quickly and easily find out who performs what function and use this tool to craft an introduction and make a connection.

CAUTION AHEAD: WORDS OF WARNING ABOUT VIRTUAL NETWORKING

Along with the ease of virtual networking comes concern about how to use these sites to portray yourself and how to determine the credibility of those you come in contact with while using the sites. For instance, given that it is a virtual world, it is quite easy for people who feel so inclined to overstate their qualifications or connections.

You have to be diligent when reviewing profiles and not get trapped by dishonest people. They only serve to waste your time and direct your focus away from where it needs to be, which is on those contacts in the virtual world who will help propel your business forward and help you meet your growth objectives. That is why it is best to do your homework and do some research on people beyond what they claim on a social networking site before you make a connection. It is often found that the more extensive a person's profile is, the less important they actually are—something that used to happen with resumes and CVs. However, individuals who are super successful and who are not looking for a job tend to have a more limited profile—that is because they are so busy they do not have time to update their profile every five minutes.

This is not meant to discourage you from virtual networking—quite the opposite. Your business depends on contacts—bottom line. Every opportunity for a meet-and-greet is essential to your business. You never know where a great contact might be found. And with virtual networking, you eliminate one step in your journey to success. Just apply common sense to your approach and use a cautious eye when dealing with unknown people.

Just as important is how you present yourself in the virtual world. You need to make sure your profile and experience are true reflections of your capabilities so you do not misrepresent yourself to others. Despite the distance often involved in virtual networking, it's still necessary to develop trust through authenticity and kept promises. Think carefully about the information you share and post, crafting an interesting and unique online profile but one that you can live up to in person and when encountering potential new clients and projects. It does not take long for word of a fraud to spread throughout the confines of the virtual networking world; it becomes nearly impossible to rebuild your reputation once your misrepresentation has been uncovered.

Those of you reading this book may already be well versed in the role of an online connection before making an in-person contact. Others of you, however, may remember the days before social networking, when you picked up the phone and made a call to see if you could wrangle a meeting or you attended a networking social to mingle and market yourself. Neither approach is wrong; if anything, combining the best of both worlds—online and offline—is the ideal strategy for today's entrepreneur. Whatever strategy you choose and that works for your objectives, the central tactic must involve making a personal connection. Here's why.

THE IMPORTANCE OF MAKING A PERSONAL CONNECTION

Just because the world has changed does not mean that virtual networking should be your only tool in the world of business contacts. It is essential to employ an offline strategy as well in order to develop the growth potential of your business fully and deepen the connections that your contacts will have with you. That is why traditional networking, which involves that face-to-face, personalized connection, still plays a pivotal role in today's world business climate—it has served as the hallmark of business interaction for centuries.

Despite the ability to reach more people in the virtual networking landscape, even with new technologies like video conferencing and Skype, it's a somewhat superficial connection that is made that cannot match the deeper emotional connection often made with face-to-face contact. When meeting in person with each other, there are non-verbal cues and actions that help you determine the character and position of your networking contact, as well as aid your connections in gauging your character. For instance, being able to gauge a person's body language, their physical reaction to a situation, the way they look you in the eye, and how they shake your hand can all be helpful in determining whether you feel comfortable working with a certain person. It is also a means of marketing yourself to others in a way that establishes credibility, professionalism, and thought leadership. It is easier to illustrate that you or your network connection is engaged and present in the relationship, which can help shape your strategy on whether the two of you will work together.

Although many of you younger entrepreneurs who are reading this book have been raised on a steady diet of online interfacing and may wonder what we are talking about, your approach to finding colleagues, investors, talent for your business, and, most important, new clients for your business cannot take place entirely online. There must be times where you meet and greet in person, carrying on casual—yet meaningful—business conversations. And these conversations do not necessarily have to be formalized within a meeting or a networking social. Networking has been conducted quite successfully for decades in other places that every entrepreneur should consider within their strategy.

Twenty-Five Best Places to Network

1. Meet-ups
2. Religious events
3. Exercise
4. Hobby clubs
5. Arts
6. Coffee shops
7. Neighborhood groups
8. Pet-related events
9. Conferences
10. Retreats
11. Ethnic- or gender-based clubs
12. Classes
13. Social media
14. Volunteer work
15. Alumni events
16. Trade shows
17. Music events
18. Chambers of commerce
19. Associations
20. Lead groups and networking events
21. Online forums
22. Blogs
23. Toastmasters
24. Speeches and talks
25. Connectors

Source: www.businesspundit.com/25-best-places-to-network/

ON PAR WITH NETWORKING: GOLF, ANYONE? HOW ABOUT A GAME OF TENNIS?

Although the "Twenty-Five Best Places to Network" table lists some of the top networking sites, a personal favorite is the golf course. Sure, many people are out on the links for the sheer joy of it, but when you spot a group out for the day, other activities are usually afoot. By that, I mean business deals are getting done in between holes and along the course. This is because when we have the opportunity to meet, socialize, and engage in casual business talk in an environment other than the boardroom or a chat room, it changes the relationship between the parties. A connection is created that is impossible to duplicate online. Camaraderie combines with serious business talk, as well as frivolity mixed with the ability to make emotional connections.

Say we partner up with a group of ten businesspeople for a game of golf or a set of tennis. Each member brings something to the game. You create a positive atmosphere based on a shared pursuit, but really you are able to use this venue to your business advantage. The talk is informal and you have the ability to gain a foothold with a business contact or secure an introduction through a mutual associate. This is priceless and can spell all the difference when securing financing for a new venture or perhaps even getting that long-sought-after lucrative contract. And in an ever entrepreneurial fashion, there are even businesses that have sprung up to take advantage of networking on the course. Fore Networking started in California as a way to organize networking events on the golf course, combining the love of the game with the desire to network and develop new business relationships. Joining a group like this or simply organizing your own networking events on the course or the court is one way to leverage the benefits of face-to-face networking while having fun.

And, like anything, face-to-face connections can have unforeseen long-term consequences. For example, Adrie played golf off and on with a gentleman for more than twenty years. They had met via business contacts and kept up a social relationship to get together and play a round of golf over the years. This same man went on to become a board member for a major petroleum company. This is a prime example of a contact that clearly might not have been possible simply by trying to contact him through a LinkedIn profile. Someone who had this much power and position would be nearly impossible to ever reach through social networking. After all, high-powered board members have a tendency not to list their e-mail addresses and phone numbers on their business cards, let alone on a company Web site or social networking profile. The point here is that you have to establish and nurture face-to-face relationships to receive value that is otherwise unavailable online.

Then there is the age factor, which is another important factor to consider when assessing the value of an offline strategy. Many important businesspeople who came of age before the Internet do not engage in or use social media—period. The contact from the petroleum company would be a case in point. This means that you have to be flexible and tailor your approach to develop your business connections fully with individuals who might not be as attuned to social networking. If you only focus on social networking, you could miss some very important connections or connectors that could lead to business growth. That is reason enough to look into some of the traditional channels mentioned previously when developing your networking strategy.

MAKING THOSE ONLINE CONNECTIONS

In looking more closely at the online channels for networking, many social media and social networking hubs are important to incorporate in your combined networking strategy. Our last chapter discussed the use of social media and the ways companies use Facebook, Twitter, E Factor, YouTube, and other online locations to increase their market share. Social media was defined as a tool we could use to transmit information to a widespread audience and also as a tool to transmit a message to the consumer via the Internet.

Where social media and social networking diverge is that point where action, dialogue, and engagement occurred within the social networking realm versus social media. Social networking is motion. Simply put, social networking is a verb! It is an action unto itself, whereas social media can be viewed more as a noun because it is more of a place to send and receive messages.

As such, sites like Foursquare, LinkedIn, and Google+ offer the opportunity to engage our customers continually with dialogue, meet prospective clients and colleagues, and network with other like-minded individuals, all to our company's benefit. Here are some brief descriptions to help familiarize those of you who might be unaware of these key online networking channels:

- **Foursquare:** Foursquare is a social networking site where people use their mobile phones to note their location and are awarded points when they log in. Users can also gain the status of mayorship, badges, and a super-user designation. Now where your company comes into play is that Foursquare offers businesses the ability to claim their business, create special offers, and connect and engage with Foursquare's millions of users for free. And we all know there is nothing better than free advertisement and promotion of our product. Therefore, using a site like Foursquare provides startups with the opportunity to connect with potential customers, advertise their sales and merchandise, and get the word out about their venture. Any way you can connect with a potential customer will increase your business presence and develop your brand.

- **LinkedIn:** LinkedIn enables users to connect with business associates, gain access to shared colleagues, and network within the confines of LinkedIn's site. You can increase your market share, establish additional business contacts, and develop revenue through a series of contacts made from shared associates. The whole movement of social networking gives entrepreneurs daily access to prospective capital funding, a nest of potential clients, and a chance to broadcast their business and brand to a wide range of people.

We often speak to entrepreneurs about their success with LinkedIn. One E Factor client, who also uses LinkedIn, related how she regularly receives work from recommendations she gets through colleagues on LinkedIn. She noted that these particular projects might have never reached her had it not been for the virtual network she had with her global connections on LinkedIn. Similarly, this is how a startup or existing business can harness social networking and use a site like LinkedIn to further their business. You can easily start with colleagues, former classmates, neighbors, and associates as a way to build a network of contacts. As you develop these contacts, you can watch as the tentacles of connections reach further out and capture a wider audience.

- **Google+:** Google+ is still an emerging site and its potential for business applications remains uncertain at the time of publication. However, what is certain is the influence of Google. It has become a power-house and a force to be reckoned with so that its potential to create a social networking site where you can develop your business is almost certain.

AN ONLINE AND OFFLINE STRATEGY FOR NETWORKING

Social networking sites can be used by developing startups and existing businesses alike. However, caution is still required when using them in a strategy. Be sure to choose wisely. It is not necessary to participate in every possible online Web site, community, and network available. If you do, you are simply spreading yourself too thin and not achieving anything produc-tive by doing so. Multiple sites can be difficult to manage and they will lose their effectiveness without proper updates and maintenance.

Instead, try to focus on two or three sites and then develop your profile fully and engage within those sites. This means updating the content regularly and using consistent messaging across the networking sites. Be sure to set aside time to par-ticipate in online events and forums so that you can meet and interact with the people you are seeking relationships with by using a virtual networking strategy.

The same can be said for your offline strategy. You cannot participate in all twenty-five channels and have any time to operate your business or cultivate those new networking contacts. Select one or two channels to participate in offline regularly and then add a couple more throughout the year that could lead to more contacts. See where there are linkages in networking opportunities between offline and online channels. For instance, E Factor is set up to cater to activities in both channels, which could help maximize your networking efforts.

SETTING THE MOOD: A NEW BAROMETER TO GAUGE YOUR BUSINESS INDEX

As new types of networking channels have opened, entrepreneurs must address a need for a new approach and strategy. We have developed a means to connect a company's relationship to social networking with its value on a daily basis. We coined the term *The E Factor Index*, which allows entrepreneurs to gauge different moods. Entrepreneurs can assess the mood of their core audience, the market as a whole, and their individual mood.

For instance, we have our members rate their feelings about business on a sliding scale of 1 to 100 every day. Much like the NASDQ or NYSE, it tracks the value and determines whether your stock goes up or down on any given day. This gives entrepreneurs a voice and a way their individual concerns and worries can be heard. Eventually, we hope to publish their number alongside other indexes in the financial papers. This will tie into a real-world application and become a measurable tool for businesses and consumers.

SEEKING OUT STRATEGIC BUSINESS CONNECTORS

Whether you seek them online or offline, one of the best strategies is to align yourself with powerful strategic business connectors. These are people who have their own established and comprehensive networks and open them up to you, working as your advocate to get you connected to others who could help you in some way with your business objectives. It might be connecting you to an investor, a potential client, or a strategic partner. They are willing to do this because they were most likely just like you at one point—a burgeoning entrepreneur—and now they want to "pay it forward." They may also have an ulterior motive that is really positive—they recognize that by helping you, you may help them in turn at some point and they see it as a way to widen their own network of connections.

Here are some of the ways they can serve as a connector for you. They can connect you to:

1. **Coaches.** Coaches are excellent contacts because they can guide and mentor you on starting and nurturing your business, including establishing a strategy with tactics and metrics.
2. **Experts.** You might not be able to do everything necessary to launch or grow your business. That means calling on experts who have the core skill sets to handle

certain aspects of a business. Getting connected to the best in a field or specialty area goes a long way toward strengthening the foundation of your business.

3. **Unbiased Opinions and Advice.** When a business idea is your baby, you can be too close to it and too emotional about it. That is when you could use connections to those unbiased opinions and advice that may help you see more clearly what you need to do or how to proceed.

4. **Capital.** Whether just starting out or expanding, you will most likely need to tap sources for capital. That's when it really helps to have some connectors who can speak on your behalf to their contacts. Sometimes, their word alone will get you a meeting and consideration for funding.

5. **Other Funding Resources.** In addition to capital from investors, you might need other resources, which your connector can direct you to within your community.

6. **Peers.** A connector may know other people like you who they feel might align with your strategic thinking or interests, helping to connect two people who can compare notes, commiserate, and share ideas to bolster both businesses.

7. **Strategic Partners.** Sometimes, you need more than temporary experts or counselors to work with, so a strategic business connector might actually be able to line up strategic partners to work within your business for a piece of the action.

8. **Top Talent.** Finding talent, the most valuable resource for your business, can be challenging. Although a large crowd of potential workers is clamoring for work, there might not be many faces in that crowd that are right for you and your business. Having a connector

who can bring you the top of the class and recognize the best talent for your business is an incredible advantage.

9. **Potential Clients.** Although the access to investors, experts, advisors, resources, and talent is an extraordinary advantage of working with a connector, you need to grow and generate profitability—and, for that, you need clients and more of them in the pipeline. Here again, a connector can bring you clients or point you toward those they think will be interested in what you have to offer.

10. **Exposure.** Like a walking billboard for your business, a connector can not only get you clients but can help you develop your image, identity, and brand within your target markets. Perhaps they even have expertise related to media, public relations, marketing, and online social media. Being able to connect with someone so savvy can generate the viral attention you are seeking to launch or grow your business.

BRINGING IT ALL TOGETHER

Combining the tools of social media and social networking will unite two distinct yet connected forces to fuel your business and drive revenue. Virtual networking can deliver results and bring an increase in market share and brand recognition while traditional networking can add the personal touch that is so necessary for nurturing new business relationships. Your job is to learn how to merge these two ideas effectively and use each one to its full potential.

KEY POINTS TO REMEMBER

- Virtual networking through LinkedIn, Foursquare, Google+, Facebook, and other sites has offered a much more expansive territory that is ripe with networking opportunities to grow your business and expand your access to funding, information, advice, talent, and, most important, customers.

- You must not sacrifice traditional networking and focus solely on virtual networking. Much can be said for the face-to-face interchange of ideas and the building of trust through handshakes, eye contact, and personal and non-verbal communication. Many deals and connections would not be made online that have been made in person.

- Consider all channels as a networking opportunity— from the golf course to a cross-country flight. You never know whom you will meet and how you might be able to help each other through sharing and collaboration.

- E Factor was designed and developed as the ultimate networking environment for entrepreneurs, combining virtual and traditional networking events and channels to maximize the ability for entrepreneurs to share information, find funding, create projects, launch ideas, and achieve great success.

NEW WORKING ENVIRONMENTS: COLLABORATION ON A CLOUD

IT SEEMS LIKE EVERY day brings a new way to communicate with colleagues, customers, and partners. We are instantly tuned in and hooked up. Whether that means a new device or a new channel, communication technology is clearly advancing at a rapid pace. Tools like Skype, free conference calling, text messaging, and video conferencing have forever altered the way we conduct business. Although it is all amazing—and sometimes overwhelming—there are advantages and challenges we must consider before plunging into all this new technology.

As each new service pops up and seemingly takes over, it is easy to understand why businesses tend to jump aboard and attempt to use these tools. However, companies can become overwhelmed with their options and lose sight of effective communication skills, which are still paramount when conducting business. That is why, as entrepreneurs, we have to be tuned in to these changes and understand how to use these devices and channels to grow our business opportunities and interact with those who will help us achieve our objectives. Therefore, our goal should be to use these tools effectively to enhance the way we communicate, network, and share information.

TOOLS OF THE TRADE: THE LATEST BELLS AND WHISTLES

To help you understand how you can use these tools, here is a brief overview of the latest bells and whistles that are changing how we communicate as entrepreneurs with our stakeholders:

- **Skype:** Skype is an application that allows users to video-conference over the Internet. Skype-to-Skype calls are typically free, but a fee is charged for mobile phones and landline usage. The advantages of using Skype are evident (free calling between Skype members!) while the setup is typically user-friendly and can provide businesses with instant communication across the globe. Now those contacts you have made on the other side of the globe can see and talk to you when and how they like, keeping the lines of communication open.
- **Google Documents:** Google's latest brainchild offers real-time online collaboration, where users can create and share documents for free. Google Docs offers a

suite of products that are stored online, in addition to revisions to prevent the loss of any valuable documents. Windows Microsoft Office, versions 2003, 2007, and 2010 can plug in with Google Cloud Connect and store Microsoft PowerPoint presentations, Excel spreadsheets, and Microsoft Word documents in either Microsoft Office or Google Docs formats. Google Docs' accessibility and lack of cost have made it increasingly more popular. However, companies should exercise great caution when using Google Docs if they are concerned about data breaches that could lead to the loss of sensitive information. Confidential information could possibly be compromised from this online document storage center so it is essential to have security measures in place.

- **Dropbox:** Dropbox is a cloud storage file hosting service that allows users to share folders and files in collaboration with other users by using file synchronization. There are mobile and desktop applications along with multiple operating system versions. Each gives your business the opportunity to work online in a collaborative environment with multiple people.
- **Cisco Systems:** Cisco offers one of our favorite interfacing technologies to date. One of their programs allows you to sit at your own conference table and fuse with another table on the other side of the world. It gives the effect that you are in the same room. Their technology even goes as far as to allow you to hear sounds from whatever angle they are coming from, just as though you were sitting around the same table. We believe that, as technology advances, it will continue to become a

more natural setting as Cisco and others continue to improve their offerings.

WHAT IS A CLOUD ANYWAY?

You might have heard about cloud computing but might not be quite sure what it means. It can actually be defined many different ways:

- **Storage Service:** Cloud computing is a storage service for information, such as photographs, files, movies, and songs. It is a great way to store large files without using up space on your computer. Plus, it makes this information accessible to as many people as you would like. This is a convenient way to share files and documents so anyone on a team can access them, or simply to access information while traveling or away from your main computer. Flickr is a good example of a cloud computing service, a place to share and store photos and images.
- **Platform:** Although operating systems have always been attributed to computers or laptops and maybe even smartphones, cloud computing can be viewed as an operating system for the Web. Serving as a platform, it is the framework for handling various applications. Examples would be Buzzword and Google Docs, just to name a couple. These could begin to replace what once was the standard application for offices and homes, allowing users to say good-bye to Microsoft Office.

Although it is still in development and has a long way to go before it becomes the new standard for communication and collaboration, cloud computing is a prime example of how the business world is continuing to change with the advances in technology.

ADVANTAGES OF NEW COMMUNICATION TOOLS

The advantages of working in real time across the globe can increase your productivity, drive your revenues, and create influence among your peers. In addition, you can gain value with these techniques for a greater sense of collaboration to boost your entrepreneurial capabilities:

- **Networking:** Real-time video-conferencing gives you an edge and allows you to work with associates across the globe.
- **Team Building:** You have the advantage of amassing talented employees and associates from a pool of applicants and organizations. You are not limited to local talent, which means that you can assemble a cross-functional team to enhance your organization.
- **Brainstorming:** There is still no better way to come up with solutions than to bounce ideas off colleagues and associates to achieve a common goal and generate diverse ideas that complement and boost your company profile. Now you can do it virtually and collect ideas from around the world.

- **Communicating:** Virtual collaboration lets you carry on a casual conversation about a wide range of daily activities and issues that affect your business and your bottom line. This allows you to work effectively with independent contractors, vendors, and telecommuting staff, just as you would if you were holding staff meetings in a physical locale.
- **Agendas:** Online communication allows the handling of project planning and execution in a simplified and straightforward manner. This can even be viewed as a more efficient process because people tend to stick to their agendas more often in a virtual world than might occur with face-to-face meetings where processes can get derailed when people go off on tangents.

By being aware of the advantages of online collaboration, you can increase your communication among your peers, associates, and business contacts across the globe and at home. Virtual collaboration eliminates the need for physical proximity for companies to conduct business. We are evolving to the point at which it is becoming common never to meet an associate in person, yet to work together as a team. You might already be enjoying these benefits.

The E Factor team already is putting this type of collaboration to work. A great example is E Factor's Made for China Startup Competition. This student-oriented business plan competition has a focus on China, providing coaching, connections, and cash prizes for startups across the globe interested in developing the Chinese market. The mission of the Made for China Startup Competition is to promote understanding of the Chinese market while building skills among young entrepreneurs. The collaboration across borders and on a virtual level is evident in the sponsorships. For instance, the financial sponsor is the Yangzhou Government of China, the technical sponsor is Cisco Systems, and the media sponsors are Tech2IPO and AngelCrunch.

This really demonstrates how advanced we are becoming and offers a little insight into where we are headed. The challenge will be to model these advancements and use them to deliver quantifiable results for your organization. Keep your eyes open to the pitfalls of these advancements and use them to your best advantage.

WHAT DID YOU SAY?

Communication tools are just that—tools to be used to enhance your ability to communicate. They should never replace your ability to interface with a client and develop a relationship. This is not to say that these tools do not have a place in your life. They do, but the trick is to see how they supplement your ability to communicate effectively, not replace it.

Face-to-face communication can never be completely replaced by video conferencing, texting, or Skype. The value of personal interaction cannot be overstated. The human connection is still important. You can build a solid reputation with personal contact and meetings to increase your business opportunities.

But this is not to say that instant communication lacks value—quite the opposite is true. Instant communication in its many forms has definite value.

The protocol of communication has evolved. We are faced daily with e-mail and text messaging, which at times can be ambiguous. Words can lose their meaning within the confines of an electronic message and a sense of formality can often be lost.

A recent situation in which a twenty-five-year-old associate sent an e-mail to a sixty-five-year-old CIO offers a prime example. The e-mail, which was positively cringe-inducing, was read aloud in the boardroom. The e-mail's language was brief, the grammar was sloppy, and the author sounded like he was writing to his college buddy rather than the CIO of a massive global organization. The moral of this story is to exercise caution to avoid losing the effectiveness of our communications through forgetting who the audience is. E-mail and texting tend to take the form of quick notes, where all the rules of grammar and punctuation are thrown out the window. But it is important to remember that this type of communication is being used in a business setting. That means that a Fortune 500 executive does not want to see "LOL" in your e-mails.

The same effectiveness message holds true in terms of communication and body language. Many misunderstandings from electronic messages are related to their lack of visual cues. The tone of voice, an arched eyebrow, or sly sarcasm can convey as much meaning as the spoken word. However, these tools are lost with e-mail and texting. Suddenly, intent can be misconstrued and you've created a disagreement or caused offense just because of the words you selected for the e-mail or text. Effective communication depends on more than words; your body language and vocal inflections can carry as much weight as the words you speak. Similarly, your written words can have many meanings and might not necessarily be understood the same way you intended them. Spend some time considering the recipient's age, background, and personality and then choose your words carefully.

BUILDING A SOLID REPUTATION ONE STEP AT A TIME

The process of building a solid reputation does not happen overnight. People will not trust you instantly. It is impossible to walk into a boardroom and establish automatic credibility. Your business character is developed from references, communal networks, and colleagues who voice their opinions about your nature and standing.

There is no shortcut to achieving a well-respected reputation. This is where establishing face-to-face contact comes into play. The firmness of your handshake and the way you address people while looking them in the eye still play a pivotal role within a business culture. Trust can be established rapidly at times when there is an instant connection. This is lost with an online-only relationship. You must take the time and, if logistics permit, develop face-to-face relationships with your business associates and partners. Your reputation will grow and you will form deeper connections within the business community.

KEY POINTS TO REMEMBER

- Communication technology is constantly evolving, and you must be at the forefront to manage your internal goals and agendas effectively within your organization.
- Virtual networking comes with hidden dangers, which you must be aware of in order to combat corporate and product development theft.

- Words can lose their effectiveness and meaning without the context of physical presence to convey their full meaning.
- Remember your audience and setting at all times to project a professional appearance with colleagues and associates.
- Trust must be earned and developing face-to-face relationships can increase your chances of establishing a rapport with associates.
- The tools you use to communicate are changing and you must adapt to the new protocols and technology in order to survive and thrive within this new culture.

NEW MINDSET:
ENTREPRENEURIAL
PHILOSOPHY 2.0

TO KNOW WHERE YOU are going, you must know where you have been. Likewise, to fully appreciate the road you travel when you are building a new enterprise as an entrepreneur, it is good to consider the past first to see how far we have come. Then filter those experiences by how they might apply to current and future opportunities. With hindsight, it seems easy to regulate your reaction and respond more efficiently to obstacles and challenges faced as entrepreneurs.

By being a visionary and a willing explorer, you can exploit each and every opportunity to increase your capabilities and expand your knowledge. The right solutions will present themselves when you open up your mind and study the past first to maneuver your way through the future. This chapter explores the evolution of the entrepreneurial mindset over the last few decades to understand how the past and present thought leadership on entrepreneurship can help you.

THE TRADITIONAL ENTREPRENEUR AND THE NEW NORM

Today's entrepreneur deviates significantly from yesterday's trailblazer. The old model of business was steeped in custom, especially in Europe. You mainly dealt with sons or daughters, who took over the family business later in life. Hordes of young people were not out in the business world, taking major plunges into the market place. Instead, the ritual of passing a business down from generation to generation was commonplace.

Adrie was a prime example of an entrepreneur who broke with this tradition. He had been working for a firm that went bankrupt, so he made the decision to go into business for himself. Adrie went to the bank and borrowed $50,000 and launched his own company. This was almost unheard of in Europe at the time. It was as though the whole idea of a lifetime family business passed down from generation to generation was the only way to go. For Adrie—and for many others who slowly appeared on the entrepreneurial scene—it was time to make a break with tradition, forge one's own path, and create a new set of rules.

THE IMPETUS FOR CHANGE

Many of today's hottest companies are simply the product of technical people who are selling their own skills and services to major companies. There were computer programmers in the 1970s and 1980s who were being hired by major banks and, in a relatively short amount of time, these same banks were asking for a steady stream of programs and applications. Of course, a lightbulb went on and some of these programmers began businesses. This change in mindset from working for a company and starting a business was the entrepreneurial mindset in action, and it accounted for the wave of small technology companies that began to appear in the late 1970s and early 1980s.

This is a far cry from the more traditional path to entrepreneurship where you would follow in your father's footsteps and take over the family business—this was a whole new wave of entrepreneurs starting businesses from scratch. And once the mold was broken, there was really no turning back. Today's entrepreneur model takes a break from tradition, migrating from a more production-based market to a service industry model. This has significantly altered the route many entrepreneurs take to achieve business success. Increasingly, there is this shift to a service-based model, where it is not uncommon for an entrepreneur to start a carpet cleaning company, perhaps with little capital outlay, and, in a relatively short period of time, see a positive cash flow.

The same is true in other service industries. There is great potential for monetary success without committing a significant capital outlay. With traditional models focused on agriculture, production, and retailing, large amounts of upfront funding were needed, especially on the retail end, where lots of capital is necessary to stock shelves with merchandise and provide the cash flow to handle significant overhead expenses. Today's entrepreneurial businesses, as you may know, do not require much to get started, which means achieving success without investing $500,000. Entrepreneurs are turning increasingly to these businesses to garner a share of the marketplace. This is an entrepreneurial mindset that has refocused on service-based businesses toward which experts see the entire world moving rather than languishing on more capital-intensive businesses.

FORGING A NEW MENTAL PATHWAY

With this change in mindset now in progress, the question you might be asking is: *How do we create opportunities working within the model we have?* The answer lies in expanding the existing model to accommodate your goals and agendas. Now this can seem a little scary, but to succeed we have to be willing to stretch and grow as individuals.

Having an entrepreneurial mindset allows you to embrace challenges and endure in even the toughest setting. However, not everyone has this mindset because not everyone who calls him- or herself an entrepreneur necessarily is one. This can put a lot of stress on people who are not equipped to be entrepreneurs. The hard fact about entrepreneurship is that only 3 or 4 percent of companies receive the capital funding they are seeking; you must be prepared to perform at this level. Bootstrapping is the name of the game when you are starting up and when there is no money and you have to prove yourself time and again. This can put an undue load on a person not prepared for the rigors of entrepreneurship.

Although people talk about balancing one's personal and work life, working as an entrepreneur and having a balanced life do not go hand in hand. With entrepreneurship, there is no balance because you are living for entrepreneurship rather than dividing your time between a professional and personal life. These are one and the same to an entrepreneur. You have to have the drive and focus to perform at an elevated level. You cannot rest on your laurels when things are changing at the speed of light. You cannot take a break from growing your business. You cannot turn off your phone and unplug the computer because that is an entrepreneur missing opportunities in the making. There is no way around this if you want to compete in today's market. So for those of you who are truly willing to call yourselves entrepreneurs, you will need to work on making some changes to your character and your skill set.

DEVELOPING NEW TRAITS

When thinking about what it means to expand the traditional role of entrepreneurship, it is important to look at our own social responsibility, how we incorporate our long-term perspective, and the ways we integrate environmental and financial performance to appease an ever-changing set of consumer demands and interests. Like many things in life, sometimes pieces fall together in an organic way to complete a cycle. Here are some different venues that combine to fill an expansive role within entrepreneurship:

- **Environmental Angle and Social Responsibility:** With entrepreneurship, it is our opinion that social entrepreneurship is sparked by the environment. You are either brought up a certain way and feel an obligation to contribute and give back or you do not. The belief in social entrepreneurship is more of a character trait driven by an internal motivation. So this is where the expansion of the traditional role of the entrepreneur is developed. It is the idea that an entrepreneur has an obligation to help other people and increase awareness with a variety of issues. This is paramount to developing new traits and expanding the traditional boundaries of entrepreneurship. Consumers today expect companies to be socially aware and conscious of today's issues and perform to increase awareness and support causes dear to their hearts. You, as an entrepreneur, can gain considerable ground in terms of credibility and trust with your target audience by illustrating your own social consciousness.

- **Financial Performance:** Capabilities are available today in terms of access to financial markets and loans. You have access to money to build your capital fund to increase your market share, develop your product lines, and decrease your time to market. E Factor is a good example of what is possible. Our ability to become a global company with just two people was possible because of the Internet. Prior to the Internet, this might have been very difficult if not impossible. The same goes with distributing products and services. There is an ease with this type of distribution that was just not there fifty years ago. The bottom line is that all these changes impact our financial performance and how we develop as entrepreneurs. This ease of use, if you will, unleashes the potential in people and allows them to develop into entrepreneurs.

THE SHAPING OF A GENERATION

This generation of entrepreneurs is forging a new path, based on pushing the boundaries of the limitations created for them. They will increase their knowledge and market share by being willing to think outside the box and compete on a different level than their predecessors. Regardless of your age and experience as an entrepreneur, you need to prepare yourself mentally for ongoing changes and remain passionate and committed to your desire to forge new business opportunities and alter the course of the global business environment.

KEY POINTS TO REMEMBER

- The entrepreneurial mindset has changed somewhat, thanks to new technology and tools now available. They provide the impetus for convincing more people that pursuing their own business dreams and ideas is possible beyond family businesses and mom-and-pop shops.
- The mindset of business is also moving from a manufacturing and retail base to service-oriented industries that are more flexible and easier to change and manage in the long term. Also, the service structure is more amenable to the shrinking business environment and societies that have been globalized and drawn together through the online movement.
- New traits are required that focus on financial performance, strategic forethought, and social responsibility. These need to be incorporated into all business startups and existing businesses as a way to sustain

them, as well as a way to attract business partners, talent, and customers.

- Younger entrepreneurs should not cast prior traits and business etiquette aside because many of those whom you seek to work with are from traditional business generations. These people still expect certain formal structures and behaviors when transacting business and communicating. That means staying professional in written and verbal communications, as well as in manners and attitude.

NEW TRANSITIONS:
FAILURE CASE STUDIES ON WHAT WENT WRONG

WHEN TALKING ABOUT ENTREPRENEURSHIP, it cannot be all about success. After all, failure happens to everyone at some point in his or her life. That is not a bad thing; if anything, it is something to learn from as you go forward. Even entrepreneurs with a great idea or product, sufficient capital backing, and tremendous drive have failed. This is simply part of the cycle of business. By being aware of failure and examining various situations where things have not gone as planned, you can better understand how to avoid going off track or how to see failure in a different light.

A CONTEXT FOR MISSING THE MARK

There are many different reasons why entrepreneurs fall short. It might be a lack of adequate funding to get their idea off the ground, their product distribution system might have had flaws, or the initial passion that drove the entrepreneur to succeed in the first place might have simply evaporated. Whatever the case, when you have a situation with an entrepreneur failing, it is important to use the luxury of hindsight to examine the possible causes and critique them. Learning about failure and seeing where other businesses went wrong can help you avoid the same fate. Today, more than ever, it is critical to be aware of all possible obstacles and challenges that might impede your success.

When evaluating the concept of "failure," don't make the mistake of thinking that all companies, and therefore all failures, are created equally. Each has a different history, agenda, and spreadsheet, which must be viewed critically and critiqued on a different level. There is no comparison between a small startup and a large corporation like General Motors. The obvious differences are that a company like General Motors has significant corporate assets as well as a sense of "they are too big to fail." This also paves the way for the federal government to intervene and offer whatever assistance is needed to prop the company up until they can reorganize and regain their footing to keep that feeling alive.

In contrast, the fledgling entrepreneur does not normally have access to vast sums of capital to keep the company afloat during a difficult period, so we need to be careful when we evaluate failure. With only 3 to 4 percent of new businesses receiving funding and operating as an untested company with little history, the focus needs to be a fair evaluation based on the merits. Therefore, when evaluating what went wrong, a category and value must be assigned to the various types of entities.

FINANCIAL MISSES AND SHAMBOLIC PERFORMANCES

Factors can work separately or merge together to form an arena where we are certain to fail. Your goal is avoid these pitfalls and maneuver around obstacles and challenges that you meet. Here are some prime examples of what not to do, starting with a recent poor example of receiving significant investment funding with the goal of financially stimulating the U.S. economy while addressing green energy initiatives. Sounds good, right? It did to the federal government when it forked over a large amount of taxpayer money to Solyndra.

You may remember that they were a Palo Alto, California, solar energy firm that received a $535 million loan guarantee from the U.S. government. In addition, it has been reported they received upwards of $1 billion in venture capital from such high-profile names as Virgin Group founder Richard Branson, Redpoint Ventures, and the Walton family, heirs to the massive Walmart fortune. Solyndra's collapse has gained the attention of the American media and led to renewed lack of confidence by the investment community in backing new ventures.

Here it was that, despite being in a high-growth market with sizable potential, the company did not think through its business strategies and address its barriers in the appropriate way. Instead, they burned through a significant amount of money in a relatively short time without having a market-ready product that could compete. It is a prime example of why you may have a more challenging time getting money through government programs as well as from investors if you do not have the strategic framework and quantifiable metrics in place.

Another major player in the high-tech market made a colossal error in judgment when they announced they were selling off their multibillion-dollar hardware division. Hewlett-Packard (HP) made this announcement only to reverse their decision weeks later and proclaim they were keeping their hardware division. Well, which one is it? Are you selling or not? Companies never want to be seen as wishy-washy, and this showed a major lapse of judgment from a giant in the industry. They single-handedly devalued a significant portion of their business. They had loyal customers and companies that were looking to other firms to supply their hardware. This is not a smart move; you never want to give your competition an edge and invite your customer to go check them out, which is just what HP did.

After the flip-flop in decision-making, the new CEO of HP announced they had decided to keep that hardware. But by now it was too late to salvage their reputation. This was a significant error that destroyed a lot of the company's value. You got the sense that no one had thought it through and evaluated the merits of the plan. This was as close to failure as you come without stepping over the line and falling into the abyss. Because once you fall, there is the real possibility you cannot get back up.

LEARNING FROM OUR MISTAKES

One of the most important questions we can ask ourselves is, "Did you learn something from this failure?" The chance of making the same mistake decreases with each experience. With luck, we can steer away from disaster if we learn from earlier mistakes.

Unfortunately, many people do not learn from their mistakes because they are too arrogant to admit they have made a mistake. Even more intriguing is a newcomer taking over from a stronger incumbent party. Many examples come to mind. Take, for instance, the U.S. Postal Service, which has announced its ongoing financial hardships in recent months. Yet companies like FedEx and UPS are operating fairly well in tough economic conditions and lead the industry—far above the U.S. Postal Service. Consider the incessant woes of the airline industry, in which big carriers like American Airlines are declaring bankruptcy and blaming all types of economic conditions and external forces for their failures.

Their dilemmas come down to two factors:

- **Lack of vision and not being quick to pick up on new trends in the market.**
  - For the U.S. Postal Service, this would be e-mail or the increased need to get parcels and envelopes to others soonest (or at all). For the airline industry, it would be changes in the kind of service they offer their customers.
- **The arrogance that the monopolists often show.**
  - This is reflected in the behavior and attitude of its management. They feel that "business will simply show up," which generates laziness and allows management to close its eyes, behavior that is often fatal.

Another example of this arrogance can be seen at IBM. They had an almost invincible position in the computer market, but their arrogant behavior nearly took them down. Smaller systems and laptops started to become the norm in a business environment that was shifting toward smaller teams and people working from home. IBM's systems did not cater to these flexible workforces.

This type of arrogance can also affect how customers feel when they try to communicate with companies. For instance, maybe you join a club as a member and then want to know more about its founders or even want to ask questions now and again and then get a response. For instance, I posted a question to Twitter's team more than six weeks ago and got an automated reply that they are rather busy and would get back to me. After two weeks of waiting patiently, I sent them another e-mail, saying that I would like an answer please, and I got a rude reply that said that because I had already asked that question and obviously was not patient enough to wait for them to get back to me at their own pace, my question had now gone to the back of the queue of all the other poor souls' questions. What does that mean? I have no idea how long this queue is, but I am still waiting for a courteous answer to my simple question. How hard can it be? Although Twitter is supposed to be a communications channel, one would hope they have at least the messaging part—their core existence, after all—honed into a fine-tuned process.

Then there is the all-powerful Facebook. We decided that it would be a good idea to pay a little money per day to Facebook for a limited period for advertising. There must be tons of entrepreneurs on Facebook who might want to look for a more dedicated alternative, such as E Factor, rather than wade through the hordes of other people. So we set up the daily payment, with the Facebook team urging us to get started as soon as possible, rising to the point of annoyance.

To our enormous surprise, after three months, our card statements indicated that they had been drawing twice as much money on a daily basis as we had approved *and* they continued doing so even after the time period we had approved had expired! Thinking it might be a mistake, we tried to contact them. Although we had had them chasing us every single day to set up the advertising, we now found they were not at home. By that, I do not mean that they sent us a message refuting our claim. No, they simply refused to answer our calls, messages, letters, and so on. For a social network, they seem to have a very ugly, antisocial side.

It seems as though Twitter and Facebook have forgotten the simple fact that by asking us to use the service they provide they have made us their customers. However, because consumer interaction with those companies is virtual, they seem to see us as something that merely makes their company a success, not as a customer they cannot be without. This arrogance could ultimately lead to the challenges currently seen by the experiences of the U.S. Postal Service and many airlines.

It is not just the large corporations or multinationals that can fall victim to this attitude. Small and medium-sized organizations can be just as guilty. A favorite restaurant of ours is a prime example. The staff is great, and the manager makes time for me because he sees me as a regular guest, and I like the food. However, one week I wanted to go for dinner and encountered a very different attitude. They apparently are always full at dinnertime and the hostess really did not want to waste any time being friendly when I asked for a table. Her attitude was so arrogant that I'm not sure I'll ever go back to that restaurant.

This arrogance sometimes comes from the sense that a company has some kind of exclusive hold over its customers—a captive audience, if you will. This is what happens when companies get greedy and forget about long-term relationships with their customers, preferring short-term financial gain. The result? Very simply, you lose your customers quickly, despite all the clauses in your contract that you have to start putting in to try to make it impossible for them to leave. And not only that, you now have very disgruntled customers who are using the Internet to share their bad feelings with thousands of people out there. Instead, do not assume your customer will be there with you forever.

Try to be proactive, think about your customers and how you can help them, and come up with suggestions before you are asked the question. Therefore, as a leader of an organization (particularly in the service industry), it is very important to ensure that your staff is kind and respectful, even if their message might be a negative one. If you calculate how much money each customer will cost you in terms of marketing and promotion, you would likely think twice about purposely—and stupidly—losing a client. That is the message you have to share with your personnel over and over again until they get it.

This brings the discussion back to the need for the airline industry to get a stronger competitor. (Are there any entrepreneurs reading this who have any ideas on creating a better airline?) A stronger competitor means a better, more caring airline. The indifference and arrogance of most of the current airlines is absolutely astounding, including the way passengers are treated—the phrase "nearly inhuman" comes to mind. However, a couple exceptions to this rule show signs of what an airline could—and should—become, namely Virgin or Singapore Airlines.

Speaking of Arrogance—and Wrong Moves— Netflix Comes to Mind: A Case Study

One of the more successful companies in recent years has been Netflix—that is, until they enacted a price change plan and did not think it through all the way. Here is a case study of what happened and why it all went wrong as they faced plummeting valuations and whispers about the coming demise of the company—so different from just a year earlier.

THE PROBLEM

Before July 12, 2011, Netflix, Inc. was at the top of its game. At this time, the company's online video streaming and mail-order DVD services held their highest stock values (at $304). With more than 20,000 on demand titles and 120,000 DVD and Blu-ray titles for mail-order rental, Netflix seemed to be doing everything right with their twenty-four million U.S. subscribers. On July 12, 2011, however, Netflix announced via an e-mail to current subscribers and a post on the Netflix blog, along with other media news sources, that they would be separating the streaming and mail-order aspects of their company. Pricing plan changes would be effective immediately for new customers; existing subscribers would have until September 1, 2011, to make the changes on their account.

Up to this point, Netflix charged $7.99 per month for unlimited online video streaming. For an additional $2.00 per month, subscribers could receive one mail-order DVD rental at a time. This pricing plan gave subscribers online streaming and one physical DVD rental at a time for $9.99 per month. On July 12, Netflix announced that $7.99 per month would still cover unlimited online video streaming. Customers would now have to pay an additional $7.99 per month to receive one mail-order DVD rental at a time. To receive the online video streaming services and the physical DVD rental, it would now cost subscribers $15.98 per month.

On the company's blog, Andy Rendich, Netflix's chief service and operations officer, wrote: "Netflix members love watching instantly, but we've come to recognize there is still a very large continuing demand for DVDs by mail." Rendich explained that a separate DVD plan was necessary because of the way online streaming and mail-order DVD rentals have become two very different markets in need of different marketing strategies. That being said, Netflix reorganized the structure of their pricing plans in order to better cater to their customers by offering their "lowest price ever for unlimited DVDs."

The response was not what Netflix had hoped for from its perceived loyal following.

THE CUSTOMER RESPONSE

It is impossible to know the response Netflix got to the e-mail that was sent to existing service subscribers regarding the changes to the pricing plan. The use of Netflix's blog, however, allows for a pretty accurate assessment of people's attitudes and reactions toward the changes. Twenty-four hours after the announcement, the first reaction comment was posted, followed by a flood of other readers agreeing with already posted comments or posting thoughts of their own. There were 12,849 Facebook comments and 5,000 blog comments—the maximum number of comments allowed on a single post. The blog post was also retweeted 4,349 times and liked a grand total of 64,000 times.

The first Facebook-connected comment on Netflix's blog post announcing the pricing plan changes was made by Willie

Williams. The points Williams mentioned seemed to represent a general trend among angered customers: "Individually your DVD and streaming services do not offer enough to justify their expense." His comment also mentioned alternatives to Netflix, such as RedBox and Amazon Prime, that he would be taking advantage of. This comment was a good indicator of why feedback by way of social media can be dangerous; his comment garnered 1,877 likes and 139 comments. The public aspect of social media allows for the rapid spread of opinion. The centrality of opinion on one interface, such as the thousands of comments on Netflix's blog post, makes it simple for an uninformed reader to understand the basic attitude toward a subject.

Aimee Avery commented on the aggregate negative attitude toward Netflix's decision when she wrote, "You've managed to pretty much piss off all of your customers, including me!" Avery also stated that she plans on becoming "even more friendly with my local RedBox. It may not deliver to my mailbox, but given that I have to go to the grocery store to get the popcorn, I'll go ahead and get my movies there too!" This comment shows that the dangers of competitors are real for Netflix and it seems that customers are willing to forsake Netflix services based on the principle of the issue. A Blogger.com member commented, "How exactly is this the 'lowest prices ever'? Not only are you slapping existing customers in the face with a fairly significant price increase, but you're outright lying about it too." The basic principle here is that customers are not ignorant: the bottom line is that they will now have to pay $15.98 for a service for which they were once paying only $9.99. Clearly, existing Netflix subscribers are aware of the blatant price increase and are not content. Given that there are other options (RedBox, Amazon Prime, Blockbuster, Hulu Plus), Netflix no longer has a competitive edge.

Netflix's subscribers also commented on the pricing plan change on the Netflix Facebook page. The post announcing that the online video streaming and mail-order DVD services would now be separate included a link to the blog post. The Facebook post got 81,821 comments—mostly outraged customers. The post was also shared 861 times. Unfortunately, it is not possible to see all 81,821 comments on the post—Facebook allows you to see only 40 comments. In this instance, the linking of multiple social media platforms—Netflix's Facebook page and Netflix's blog—might not have necessarily been a positive action. A Netflix subscriber sees the post on Facebook and the angry comments before they even click on the link to the blog post. After having read the blog post, more negative comments appear on the page. Although the participatory nature of social media is why companies take advantage of it in the first place, an extremely negative outcome is evident in this example. The fostering of negative feelings toward Netflix was made possible by the conjunction of multiple social media platforms.

AN ATTEMPT AT DAMAGE CONTROL

By the implementation date for the new pricing plan, it was pretty clear that customers were not pleased with the changes. In an attempt to placate angry customers (or former customers at this point), CEO Reed Hastings issued an explanation. The apology letter reached customers through a Netflix blog post, a YouTube video that also featured Andy Rendich, a Facebook post that connected users to the Netflix blog, and an e-mail that was sent to current subscribers.

The Netflix blog featured a new post on September 18, 2011, titled "An Explanation and Some Reflections," written by Netflix CEO Reed Hastings. He began by saying, "I messed up. I owe everyone an explanation." Hastings went on to say, "It is clear from the feedback over the past two months that many members felt we lacked respect and humility in the way we announced the separation of DVD and streaming, and the price changes." The post is more of an explanation of why Netflix decided to implement the new changes. The reasons behind the price change decision included trying to keep up with new innovations (online streaming), attempting to make DVD by mail "last as long as possible," and improving each branch of their services. Throughout the post, Hastings continually repeated that he should have communicated the change better by providing a personal justification for why the changes were occurring.

Hastings also took this opportunity to announce that the split in price for each service would be reflected in a split within the company; the DVD-by-mail service would become its own entity and be renamed Qwikster. The advent of Qwikster would entail an entirely different Web site. Users would have to register separately on Qwikster.com, pay their bills separately, and movie ratings would not transfer over. The same information was relayed in a YouTube video in which Reed Hastings and Andy Rendich took turns justifying their actions. All the same points were addressed, with a lot of emphasis put on the fact that it was the poor communication between Netflix and its customers that was the root of the outrage. The e-mail apology was yet another reiteration of the same message.

CUSTOMER RESPONSE TO THE EXPLANATION

Again, Netflix saw an overwhelming response to their latest proclamation. More than 27,700 Facebook-connected comments were made on the Netflix blog explanation post and it seems as if comments from Blogger.com users were disabled on this post. The post was retweeted 5,036 times and 58,000 people liked the post. One theme that appeared in angry customer comments was that the explanation was a fake apology. In Zachary Oden's long and fuming comment on the Netflix blog, he wrote that the real issue he had with Netflix was the "false sense of placation" that Netflix was attempting with their "Guilt-induced, pseudo-humble [message]." Not only did Oden feel belittled by the explanation, but it made him even angrier. The comment goes on to say, "The public is hyper-aware of their entertainment options, and any bullshit that might entail will quickly be streamlined, or better yet, jettisoned completely." The post had 847 likes and 66 comments that mostly praised Oden's point of view.

Another theme that emerged from the comments on the blog post was that Netflix had ultimately complicated the user experience. Regardless of price plan changes, Brian Wilkens felt that it was now harder to use Netflix's service. He says, "The flow of my interaction with your brand is getting more complicated, and all the trends are in favor of simplicity." Wilkens also reminded Netflix to "remember the user." Even if the customer could afford or was still willing to pay the price increase, the service Netflix was now providing was ultimately weakened.

The Netflix Facebook page post had 11,030 comments and was shared 816 times. Similar reactions were voiced on the Facebook post as were seen on the Netflix blog. The 4,089 comments in reaction to the YouTube video were perhaps the nastiest of all the responses. Comments like "Do you really think we believe your apology with that little smirk on your face. All you see is dollar signs!" and "He's not sorry. He was smiling when he said it. It's a joke" show the increasing amount of animosity. Clearly, all of these attempts to "make nice" with

Netflix customers were backfiring. It should be noted that there was no announcement of the explanation post on any of Netflix's Twitter accounts. Netflix, however, does have multiple Twitter accounts—a customer service account, a Netflix Instant account, and a company account.

There is a caveat here that should be noted. Social media is special in that it allows for interaction between friends, strangers, or even national companies. In the case of Netflix, they took advantage of the sheer number of people with whom social media allowed them to connect. By connecting their company's blog with Facebook and vice versa, they allowed their content to reach an unprecedented number of people. Unfortunately, because their content was reaching so many people, the negative comments and reactions to the news could also be seen by a lot of people.

WHAT NETFLIX COULD HAVE DONE DIFFERENTLY

The interactive element of blogs and Facebook allows companies to receive a lot of feedback from customers. That being said, Netflix's announcement of changes in the operation of their company and, more important, to the cost of their services, on social media platforms allowed the opportunity to hear what their customers had to say. As has been discussed, customers' responses were not so positive. Social media, however, afforded Netflix the opportunity to address some of the concerns that their customers voiced. The flood of comments on the Netflix blog posts and the Facebook posts provided a lot of material for Netflix to work with.

Customers were upset over the price increase and the complications that the separation of the services presented. Netflix not only opted not to respond personally to angry comments but also failed to address the real issues. Netflix higher-ups issued a statement apologizing for the lack of communication between the company and its customers. The fact that Netflix issued this statement after two months of receiving comments from customers about what they were not happy about makes the explanatory blog post even more inappropriate. In no comment did a customer ask Netflix to justify or explain the price increase. If Netflix was not planning to interact with its customers, they should have issued a press release statement on the issue.

As Brian Wilkens reminded the company in his comment on Netflix's explanatory blog post, "remember the customer." In all of this available feedback, customers were saying that, beyond the price changes, they did not like the separation. For customers who could afford to pay the higher service rates (and still chose to), they would now be inconvenienced by having to go to two separate interfaces to take advantage of those services. Here was all of this feedback, essentially warning Netflix against creating Qwikster, yet Netflix forged ahead. That is, until the morning of October 10, 2011, when Netflix issued yet another blog post announcing that they would keep the online streaming and mail-order DVDs on the same Web site: "In other words, no Qwikster."

QWIKSTER PLAN CANCELLED

The announcement that "DVDs will be staying at Netflix. com" was made at 5:00 A.M. and by 10:00 A.M. there were already 327 Facebook-connected comments. The post had also already been retweeted 1,731 times. It is comforting to know that Netflix was not completely ignoring customer responses, especially given that the responses pouring in over the past two months had not only been tremendous in number but also emotional in tone. It should also be noted that current subscribers were also notified by an e-mail message. Both announcements stated not only that there would not be a separation of the Web sites, but there would not be any more price changes. The announcement, which was made by CEO Reed Hastings, also reminded customers about the constant improvements to the streaming selection.

Responses to this new installment in the Netflix saga have been split. One side of the response is grateful; they are glad that their outrage has produced action and they feel like Netflix has finally listened. One such customer, Lori Burelle, commented, "Finally, someone at Netflix listened to reason and to the customers. Now it looks like I will be staying, at least for now." Customers like Lori seemed to be placated, but as she said it might just be "for now." Her comment also states that she will be monitoring the streaming choices that Netflix provides.

This comment shows how important it is for Netflix to come through on their promise of an improved streaming selection and to continue to offer the same selections that they have in the past. One of Lori's concerns is that Netflix will "become Blockbuster" by failing to supply "indie and foreign titles." It seems as though Netflix finally did right by listening to their customers, and if they want to continue to have a positive response, they need to continue to react to what their customers are saying.

The other type of response reflected the tone of previous customer comments: they were still mad and discontinuing their subscriptions. One comment by Geoffrey Sperl says, "Sorry, Reed . . . you've already screwed yourself in my eyes." There were many comments like this that called for Reed to step down as CEO, saying that the amount of damage he had done was irreparable. And in a way it was; the change in pricing is what angered customers in the first place and the complete separation of the two services was the icing on the cake. As demonstrated by the comments, this announcement was too little, too late.

THOUGHTS ON QWIKSTER

The conception of Qwikster is interesting because it was not part of the original price plan changes but rather was announced during Netflix's explanation letter in September. I'm assuming that the separation was part of Netflix's long-term plan and that they would have implemented it after the pricing plan changes had stabilized. They obviously did not plan on such a passionate and angry customer response. To a certain extent, the separation makes sense. Two separate platforms for online streaming and mail-order DVD rental seem coherent in terms of the separation of the pricing plans. Perhaps Netflix felt customers would better accept the pricing plan change if they thought of the two different services as completely different entities.

Ultimately, this part of the Netflix drama that has ensued in the past few months has shown the importance of responding to customer feedback. As will be discussed more in the conclusion, social media provides an excellent platform for the collection of customer feedback. It is a waste to ignore it. One comment by Jon DeBoer on the blog announcement that Qwikster would no longer be materializing said, "I give you credit at least for responding to customer feedback." But does a company really need credit for responding to customer feedback? It seems like it should be an innate part of business in our age of social media.

CONCLUDING THOUGHTS ON NETFLIX

The situation that Netflix is now dealing with reveals some important aspects of the nature of social media. First of all, as has been stressed throughout, customers are not ignorant. In fact, modern consumers have the ability to stay very well informed about products, services, and companies through various Web sites and magazines (*Mashable*, *Wired*, and *Consumer Reports*). If consumers so desire, they can research the different types of online video streaming available to them in a matter of seconds. Based on the comments Netflix subscribers left, Netflix consumers are no exception; they easily see past the façade that Netflix has created.

Even though Netflix said that the new pricing plan is their "lowest price ever," it is quite visible that it is not; customers would now have to pay $15.98 for a service for which they were once paying $9.99. No matter what Netflix says or how they try to explain their business model, it does not change this fact. Social media has allowed for Netflix's futile attempts at damage control to be awfully transparent, widely transmitted, and easily quoted, commented on, and documented.

Although Netflix did not necessarily take advantage of the interactive nature of social media, their customers did. It is visible on both the Netflix blog posts and on the Netflix Facebook page that customers were interacting with other customers. For the most part, comments agreed with points raised by angered customers. In other instances, people voiced their own opinions and then referenced another comment, stating that they hadn't thought of that point on their own. Customers commented, liked, and even shared other comments.

In one instance, Andrea Scott commented, "Well said Jodi . . . and thanks for mentioning the Amazon thing, I was unaware of that option." (This comment was referring to Amazon Prime, which also allows for online video streaming.) This shows how customers were using the social media platform to seek out information and even took advice from it. The spread of ideas, especially among angered customers, fostered a sense of unity among those against Netflix. Whether or not this phenomenon has had an actual impact on the general consensus on Netflix's actions is debatable. It is, however, very clear that different customers were being guided by each other's thoughts and opinions.

Throwing the Book at Borders—What Went Wrong: A Case Study

The automatic assumption about what went wrong with Borders might seem obvious to an entrepreneur and even a consumer—bookstores do not work in the age of the Internet, let alone after the introduction of the new e-readers and tablets. And to a certain extent, that can be true of independents around the country, including the world's largest in Portland, Oregon—Powell's City of Books—who note the challenges of running a brick-and-mortar bookstore when the world is changing so rapidly. Yet, it would also be easy to think that, in a society so attuned to information and content, a bookseller would be king.

For Borders and book lovers alike, though, it was a sad day when the chain shuttered its nearly four hundred stores and laid off nearly eleven thousand employees when it liquidated its business. Although Borders placed a lot of the blame on the economy, other chains, like Barnes & Noble, have continued to operate essentially unscathed, showing that you cannot always pin your problems on the economic conditions. The argument about not staying up with the e-reader can also be discounted. Although Amazon did enter the market first with the Kindle device, Barnes & Noble was not far behind and quickly adapted its model with the introduction of the Nook.

What it comes down to is that those behind Borders long ago lost their passion and their vision for what the company could be and could offer its customers. As such, the competitive advantage it could hope for was shelved and long forgotten. It was not just the lack of competition with e-reader devices, but it was also coffee, corporate strategy, and how it viewed its presence on the Internet. Instead of handling its own e-commerce strategy and site, it outsourced these sales to Amazon, handing over its own customer base to what became a formidable competitor. Suddenly, these customers did not need Borders for their books, music, and magazines. They became Amazon customers. Meanwhile, these customers no longer saw a reason to visit a Borders store, which is where Borders had focused its entire strategy. By the time Borders took back its online presence in 2008, it was essentially too late.

Carrying on its theme of "a little too late," Borders even tried to put out an e-reader device called the Kobo. Of course, this was in 2010 and the market was already flooded with the Kindle, which debuted in 2007, and the Nook (now available in retail stores other than Barnes & Noble), the iPad by Apple, and numerous other tablet devices. Borders also tried to hop on the diversification train well after it had left the station; even then, it did not deliver a well-conceived strategy. Borders diversified into CDs and DVDs but unfortunately focused too much time and money on this part of their business. Then there was the misstep with coffee partners. Although Barnes & Noble got the favorite pick of Starbucks, Borders got stuck with the lesser-known Seattle's Best Coffee.

Finally, Borders did not think through how to handle the size and selection of its stores, which led to huge overhead costs and enormous inventory combined with shrinking sales. It opened too many stores and got stuck in long-term leases, which meant that it could not shutter poorly performing locations quickly. It became a sinking ship because the overall strategy lacked proper vision; the company even missed out on business fundamentals that any entrepreneur or multinational company would have known. Borders became the ultimate example of a major "fail."

What can be said is that retail has become a problematic business on which to focus. It comes with a complex set of rules and a growing set of challenges—that's why more businesses and entrepreneurs are moving into more service-oriented businesses that do not require large investments or the management of a large physical presence in the market. Even other currently successful companies like Barnes & Noble and completely online firms like Amazon have experienced some of the same issues. They might have more complex problems in the future, especially now that Apple and Google are starting to sell books. How they handle it will depend on their level of passion and their vision to create the solutions that will help sustain their businesses.

COMPANIES THAT THOUGHT THEY HAD A HANDLE ON SOCIAL MEDIA MARKETING . . . BUT DIDN'T HAVE A CLUE

Other companies may not necessarily be failures but simply can be defined as not being successful at what they have attempted.

Time and time again, social media campaigns by major companies illustrate missteps and the need for "do-overs" until they get it right.

The first example is Walmart's social media marketing promotion on Facebook. In 2006, Walmart launched a Facebook profile to market their merchandise to college freshmen. Their focus was on back-to-school merchandise and dorm room accessories. They wanted to recreate the same level of success as Target had when it launched its social media marketing campaigns. The public relations firm Edelman was responsible for marketing and direction of the campaign. The main premise was to develop an interactive site where college-age students could take a quiz to evaluate their decorating style and receive suggestions and advice on merchandise. The site was intended to create a place for young consumers to find merchandise and supplies for school.

There were many missteps. First, there was no interaction (something we stress is a must-have!) and a hard-sell overload. The primary principle of a social media campaign is that it will generate interaction without the need for a mediator. Instead, people should feel free to talk and share, as well as stimulate comments and opinions. However, Walmart placed restrictions on their Facebook site by disallowing discussion boards and by heavily moderating wall posts.

In essence, it felt too Big-Brotherish because consumers immediately sensed Walmart was attempting to restrict commentary. The result was negativity and a social media marketing campaign that backfired. Rather than taking a page from Target's book, Walmart went for heavy promotion and no interaction. Target allowed people to comment and upload photos and their page centered on dorm room survival tips rather than obvious marketing.

Another misstep was pretending to be something they were not. Walmart also was criticized for their futile attempt to offer advice on style and fashion. Everyone pretty much knows that Walmart is the place to go for cheap merchandise, not high fashion or sophisticated decor. This illustrates why it is important to craft your brand attributes carefully rather than pretending to be something everyone knows you are not. When users on social media sites feel companies are deceiving them, their reaction will not be the one you want. Consumers want authenticity and are tired of being lied to by companies.

There are many lessons to be learned here. Do not try to restrict the flow of information because social media sites are a place where people can exchange information without restraint. Do not try to be something you are not. If you want to change your corporate identity, develop a strategy that changes both your offline and online presence simultaneously and allow people the time to get used to the changes, such as the way Target re-engineered itself. Do not deceive people because today's consumer is savvy and knows when you are not being authentic. Finally, do not assume you know your audience. You must do comprehensive research before telling them what you think they want to hear and see.

Then there is Burger King, which made a whopper of a social media marketing mistake with its campaign titled "Whopper Sacrifice." Despite being conceived as a short-lived social media marketing campaign conducted through Facebook, it required Burger King to rethink how it approached its target audience. The campaign promised free food in exchange for dumping ten Facebook friends. Although it was attempting to be edgy and connect with the audience, the campaign made serious mistakes.

Facebook suspended Burger King over this campaign, which created negative publicity. It was an overall negative campaign based on antisocial behavior, which went against everything that social media marketing is intended to offer. Although it was just meant to be a joke, no one was laughing. A company cannot assume that everyone shares the same sense of humor and should realize that it might be offending its own audience. Also, do not assume that social media sites will comply with your campaign willingly. They will shut you down if they do not like how you are using their platform in a marketing campaign. The biggest lesson to learn is to not use a platform in a counterproductive way; that is, don't use social media for an antisocial event. It is a failure waiting to happen.

Skittles also left a bitter taste in the mouths of its customers with its attempt to use social media marketing in a way they thought would stand out. Again, this candy brand's assumptions and lack of research led to some serious missteps. The Skittles Web site was transformed into a multichannel social platform for visitors through a networking interface that allowed people to type anything they wanted. That is a recipe for disaster, especially when it became flooded with juvenile, immature content that was often inappropriate. Parents were enraged and the candy brand's parent company, Wrigley, had some explaining to do.

Unlike other examples, where too much monitoring was involved, this was an example of an effort that could have done with some moderating. There was nothing social about what was attempted and it lacked a real way to connect emotionally with the intended audience. The site provided no interaction with Skittles or anyone else for that matter. It seemed random and lacked real forethought. Overall, the campaign's lack of direction and thought about what might transpire left a bad taste in everyone's mouth.

The first lesson to be learned here is to not be lazy when it comes to your efforts to engage and interact with your audience, assuming they will do most of the heavy lifting for you.

Do not confuse or insult your audience, let alone leave them in charge of the campaign. Be sure you know your demographic and stick to it. At Skittles, no one knew whether the campaign was directed at children, teens, or adults. In the end, it did not resonate with any of those audiences.

Sony offers another example of a company that assumed it knew what it was doing and that it understood what its audience wanted. Its "All I Want for Xmas Is a PSP" campaign provided another example of a major misstep. The objective was to generate buzz with their target consumers through what they had hoped would be a viral campaign, where consumers would produce their own YouTube videos for promoting the PSP 3. A video/blog appeared featuring two young teens, Charlie and Jeremy. Charlie, who describes himself as a "playa," attempts to convince Jeremy's parents to buy him a PSP 3 for Christmas. Both teens use appropriate Internet lingo, but all is not what it appears to be. It was discovered that those behind the blog and video were actually a marketing company. Charlie and Jeremy were simply actors and it was all a fraud.

Within days, Sony sent out a public apology for attempting to fool their audience and admitted they were simply trying to be cool and clever. But they did not understand what viral campaigns were and how they happen. A campaign goes viral because people love the concept and begin talking about it and sharing it. These cannot be manufactured or contrived. They really have lives of their own and do not work any other way. When customers discover that they have been duped, they are very unhappy and take it out on the company that tried to fool them. Sony took the brunt of their customers' anger. The campaign failed and their reputation was somewhat tarnished.

Even worse, their stunt got the government involved and changed the rules of the game for how companies utilize online marketing sites. In 2009, the U.S. Federal Trade Commission (FTC) established new guidelines for online blogs so that companies must now state up front that they are providing financial support or incentive for a person or entity to provide testimony for a product. Otherwise, they will face a fine.

All of these examples share strategies and approaches that illustrate why some companies fail—or stumble—in how they market themselves, approach their customers, and handle their mistakes. Although these have all focused on online social media marketing campaigns, they illustrate specific lessons that you can apply as an entrepreneur with your own businesses or startups. You need to know your audience, engage and interact with them, and acknowledge any mistakes in how you approach them. Companies of all sizes can make mistakes like the ones outlined here, but the most important lesson is to not let these problems derail your long-term efforts. Note where you went wrong and try, try again.

THE RULES OF THE GAME

Addressing the challenges to successful businesses requires becoming better equipped to handle the obstacles thrown our way and stiff challenges we might face. Our goal is uncomplicated and straightforward, and the key to success lies within if we put together these components as the foundational blocks to our businesses:

- **Simplicity:** The art of simplicity can keep you and your business focused. Encumbering your business with complex agendas, which only muddy the waters, can bring it to its knees. Keep it simple and be succinct in everything you do.

- **Consistency:** The ability to form a business plan and develop it to its fullest potential is vested in a consistent plan. It has been the death knell of many organizations to allow new people to come in and tamper with a proven formula. The result is that they drive the company into the ground within two years by changing the rules and altering a proven formula.

- **Conceptualization:** The skill to merge and acquire a business successfully is an art form. The ability to marry different expectations and goals is essential to continuing success for a company. Many times, the founder is the driving force behind the company; when new people come on board, they may lack the orientation for detail the company's creator brought to the organization.

- **Drive:** Many companies have been caught resting on their laurels only to be overtaken and replaced by younger and hungrier organizations. A market leader like Yahoo! can be replaced by Google if they lose their focus, their drive, and their motivation.

- **Sidelined:** Keep your business consistent. Never marginalize and lose sight of your initial goal. Take, for example, a company that sold shoes. As they grew and made money, they invested in real estate. Soon, their real estate was worth more than their business and became their main focus. Eventually, their shoe business suffered because they lost sight of their core business.

By applying these principles to your business, you can avoid the dangers and maneuver your business to success.

KEY POINTS TO REMEMBER

- There is failure, there is missing the mark or a mis-step, and there is a lack of success. Remember that failure comes in varying degrees. It is all relative and tied to the type of mistake, type of business, and the reaction of stakeholders. The way in which it's handled also determines the true degree of failure or lack of success.

- Failure is a good thing if you learn from it. You need to understand what and why part or all of something went wrong. From there, you need to determine how it can be changed so you can move forward. Many a failure or mistake has led to a new and better business.

- A true failure comes when the business or leadership team does not have the right mindset. They let arrogance or the presumption of power cloud their judgment, assuming they know what customers want or that they can tell customers what they want. That no longer works as the airlines, the U.S. Postal Service, and many big-box retailers and consumer goods companies have found when they have tried to market online and offline to their target audiences.

- You need to apply a new set of principles to your business by keeping it simple, consistent, and in line with what your audience wants. It's essential to keep moving and changing, and to stay focused on your core business, never losing sight of why you created the business in the first place.

NEW TRANSITIONS:
SUCCESS CASE STUDIES OF COMPANIES ON THE MOVE

FOR THE NUMBER OF mistakes made, there are just as many success stories among entrepreneurs and today's leading companies. That is because companies on the move—growing and expanding—are those that understand that the survival of the species depends on the ability—and flexibility—to evolve and adapt to their environment. This chapter will explore how this prime character trait leads to success.

Early on, successful entrepreneurs realize that they cannot always stick with their original plans. If anything, changing the plan has actually resulted in bigger and better results than originally anticipated. After all, it does not make sense to think you can simply stick to your guns if the market changes or the competition comes up with something new. Often, you see that the most successful companies have a business plan that points them in one direction but a couple years later they are doing something completely different.

REACHING OUT FOR THE BIGGER PICTURE

These companies don't get so hung up on what the competition is doing when deciding what they should do. Instead, they focus more on how to be the best that they can be, which is something many entrepreneurs and company leaders have not yet learned to do. If you are looking over your shoulder to see what everybody else is doing, then you are not looking forward. You may stay frozen by the concern that someone else is doing a better job than you when your efforts should be focused on looking at your audience and how your capabilities can satisfy them. Of course, you do not want to ignore the competition; just do not fixate on what they are doing. You have to stick to your own vision and make that work.

Reaching out for this bigger picture also means approaching people in different ways. It might mean tweaking your social media strategy regularly as you gain a better understanding of your target audience or come in contact with networking contacts that provide you with another perspective. Although it might be easier for you to take the same route, you will forget about the landscape that is so much bigger than the small area through which you are currently traveling. It takes creativity and courage to forge that new niche path or traverse the road less traveled. But it is necessary as one of many tactics that all successful companies can say they share.

To chart your course, you need to turn to your target audience. Here are some of the questions we have asked of our target groups:

- What are you reading?
- What are you interested in?
- What is your perspective? How do you feel about X, Y, and Z?
- What are you viewing? Are you tuned in to YouTube videos? Are you constantly checking Facebook? Do you prefer LinkedIn?
- What are you using to view that content?

Although it is a constant struggle to find this right direction, especially when that direction often changes, asking these questions regularly helps to realign our strategic course.

Navigating this course also involves reviewing statistics on a frequent basis. Although tools like Google Analytics do help, you need to explore other metrics, thanks to an ever-growing toolbox of statistical tools now available:

- What do people do when they come to your Web site?
- Where do they stop and linger a while?
- What is their breaking point? That is, when do they decide they have spent enough time on your Web site?
- What effect does your Web site have on them?

These statistics will identify what is working and what is not. You also can turn to experts in this field who can figure out how to analyze these different opinions.

Case Studies on Doing It Right

Fleet Feet, Publitas, ING Direct USA, Virgin America, and Barnes & Noble are five prime examples of companies that are doing things the right way. The following section of this chapter explores how these five companies serve to demonstrate the traits necessary for entrepreneurs and business leaders alike to achieve sustainable success.

Fleet Feet

Fleet Feet, Inc. is a specialty retail store founded in 1976 in Sacramento, California, by Sally Edwards and Elizabeth Jansen. The store focuses on specialty fitness footwear, apparel, and accessories. After the store's initial success, they decided to start new franchises in different cities across the nation. Fleet Feet, Inc. was bought by Tom Raynor in 1993 and continues to be a successful network of stores, with more than 100 locations.

Fleet Feet was founded with an emphasis on the importance of community and customer relationships; the people at Fleet Feet take these principles very seriously. One of the ways that they foster customer relationships is through their Fitlosophy™, which provides all customers with an individualized and personal fitting process. The fitting process entails five steps: getting to know you, measurements, gait analysis, fitting and recommendations, and finally a decision. A Fleet Feet employee will first listen to your goals and running activities, measure your feet for size, watch you walk and run, and then bring different options for you to try on. Fleet Feet stresses that they will pick the best shoes for you—not the most expensive shoes or the flashiest-looking pair. Their emphasis is on fit, support, and comfort, not necessarily the aesthetic aspect.

Fleet Feet not only fits customers for running shoes but also helps them find the perfect fit for inserts, socks, and sports bras. Of all the special features that Fleet Feet provides, this is unique, mostly because the average running shoe customer would not know the importance of finding a good fit for these running accessories. Fleet Feet says that inserts are really important for runners because every foot and body is different and the actual running shoe can only do so much. The right insert might be crucial to provide the necessary foot support and body alignment for a runner. Socks are also an important element of running performance. A Fleet Feet employee will help customers look for elements such as seams, fibers and materials, ergonomic fit, heel pocket, needle count, and engineered cushioning. Finally, Fleet Feet can help customers find the right sports bra. They claim that more than 80 percent of women are wearing the wrong bra size, so they work to help them find a better fit that provides comfort, support, and breathability. The company really stresses the importance of people as individuals; they don't see their customers as a homogeneous group but as very different people with very different running needs.

This outlook is also reflected in Fleet Feet's health and fitness campaign: "Be the Movement." The movement really emphasizes fitness for everybody, regardless of age, current fitness level, or training goals. Fleet Feet provides different training programs for people of all skill levels; these training programs are central to the company's involvement in the community. The "Be the Movement" campaign really stresses the participation of the entire community. In the video on their Web site, Fleet Feet participants comment on how the store "is like a family" and how it is more than just a retail store because it provides a "full experience."

Another participant says how the running and training

programs are useful to him because the coaches are "extreme motivators." Others say that they appreciate the programs because "you never feel like you're alone" and that Fleet Feet "makes you feel very welcome regardless if you're a walker that is just starting running or if you've been a runner for years." This movement and the different training programs Fleet Feet offers not only get the larger community involved but provide them with an experience that is even bigger than exercise. One satisfied participant said that once she joined a Fleet Feet training program, running "stopped being exercise and it stopped being work" and instead was something that she genuinely enjoyed doing.

SOCIAL MEDIA OUTLETS

As a national retailer, Fleet Feet takes advantage of Facebook and YouTube to connect further with customers. Their Facebook account has almost 6,000 likes, and they take a very active role on the page. They create status updates frequently and have a very high level of interaction; users not only like various posts, but they comment on them. The content on the Facebook page is made up of a variety of things; content ranges from product information and promotions to running tips, congratulatory posts, and running-related news. The Fleet Feet Facebook page also has a lot of pictures that are posted both by Fleet Feet and other Facebook users. The pictures show different products and community events in order to showcase all of the different aspects of the company. Fleet Feet also has a YouTube account with more than twenty different videos that showcase various models of running shoes. The videos seem to be more promotional than anything else and a new video has not been posted in more than two months.

COMMUNITY INVOLVEMENT

All of the different Fleet Feet locations have their own Web sites. The Web site for Fleet Feet in Chicago prominently features an upcoming event, along with new products that the store just received. Judging from the emphasis of the Web site homepage, the company's priorities are still clearly present. Even though the Web site details all of the store's products, the majority of the content on the page is geared toward community events.

If you go to the events tab on their Web site, the Fleet Feet Chicago calendar shows eighty-seven upcoming events. The events range from Women's Only Events, Seminars, Fun Runs and Walks, Races, and Community Yoga. The events are free and usually just require a simple RSVP. As mentioned in the Fleet Feet, Inc. background, Fleet Feet stores all offer training programs for different levels of fitness and achievement. Fleet Feet Chicago is no different, with programs ranging from No Boundaries, a program for beginning runners, to a marathon group for those training for 26.2-mile courses.

Fleet Feet Chicago is also involved with the community through its partnership with various charities. Charities include the AVON Walk for Breast Cancer, American Cancer Society, Chicago Area Runners Association, Girls on the Run Chicago, and the Leukemia and Lymphoma Society. The charities that they choose to support not only raise money and awareness for health and social issues but help train many runners. Throughout the calendar year, Fleet Feet Chicago holds various events for these different charities.

The individual Fleet Feet retailers also seem to be much more active in their social media outlets than Fleet Feet, Inc. Fleet Feet Chicago uses Facebook, Twitter, and a blog. The Fleet Feet Chicago Facebook page has more than 6,700 likes and provides a wide variety of information. Content includes information on events, product and store promotions, and links to the store's newest blog posts. There is a lot of interaction on the Facebook page; customers comment and like the frequent status updates and even feel comfortable enough to post comments and questions on the Fleet Feet Chicago Facebook wall. All comments and questions are quickly responded to with detailed information.

One Facebook user recently posted a comment on the Fleet Feet Facebook page complimenting the great service, staff, and products. Not only is this proof of a very satisfied customer, but Fleet Feet Chicago quickly thanked the satisfied customer. Like the company's Facebook page, there are a lot of pictures that are posted by both the Fleet Feet store and Facebook users. Pictures show store employees, new products, and various events.

Fleet Feet Chicago employs a Twitter account in which they have more than six thousand followers. Again, as on Facebook, they use their Twitter account very actively and have posted more than eight thousand tweets. They usually post around five tweets per day; it is a mix of retweets, responses, and tweets about various running and Fleet Feet news. They prominently feature their Twitter account on the Fleet Feet Chicago Web site, providing a live feed and multiple links.

Finally, Fleet Feet Chicago has a blog—the link is on their Web site. The blog provides more in-depth information than both of their other social media outlets. There are usually about four posts a week, if not more. Content ranges from inspirational posts such as "Five Reasons to Run in the Winter" to educational posts such as "Post-Marathon Recovery Tips." Other posts include gear reviews, coaching tips, and nutritional guidance.

THOUGHTS ON FLEET FEET'S SUCCESS

Fleet Feet, as a retail store, does not cover half of what they do. Instead, they are more of a fitness community that aids running and other activities through the personalized sale of athletic equipment. Through their various social media outlets and Web sites, they show that the emphasis really lies on the community events, races, and training programs that are provided to customers.

In the case of Fleet Feet Chicago, they exhibit an extreme level of commitment that is reflected not only in the prominent display of event information on their Web site but in the amount of interaction on their social media platforms. Both their Facebook and Twitter pages provide a lot of relevant information to customers and fitness enthusiasts. By putting the emphasis on individuals and their fitness goals, there is less focus on the product. The high level of staff assistance that the customer receives in the store is a way to foster this community involvement. I looked on the Fleet Feet Chicago Yelp page to look at some of the reviews from various customers. Although some customers did have negative customer service experiences, the store had an overall rating of four stars. One satisfied customer describes the loyalty that she feels for Fleet Feet due to the knowledge the employees have about their products, the way that she feels included, and great customer service. The entire package—quality products, expert advice, and training programs/events—provides a lot of value to customers. This value is reflected in a high level of customer loyalty that is ultimately one of the secrets to Fleet Feet's success.

Fleet Feet is more than a retailer; they are building a community around their store by organizing events, holding running workshops, and delivering excellent service. They really distinguish themselves from other stores by following up with you. Fleet Feet really goes beyond what you would expect from a store and they are very well integrated into the community in a very active way, which sets them apart from most other stores.

The reason they are so different comes down to the attitude of their management. Essentially, they feel that what they are doing is simply what they should do. It is not just that they should run a store and make money doing it; it is about becoming an integral component of the community. The management imbues this philosophy in everything they do so that it is passed on to everyone who works for them, which is then passed on to the shoppers in hopes that they carry that attitude into whatever they do in their own personal and professional lives. It is like the retail version of "pay it forward." Finally, what is most interesting is that Fleet Feet is a relatively small organization, although they do have a nice network of shops. What you see with their bigger stores is that they use social media mainly for special offers. This is a total communication effort with their customers and potential customers, and it is far beyond what so many retailers offer today.

Publitas

The next success case study is the Dutch e-publishing company Publitas. They illustrate the innovative ways that various social media platforms can be incorporated into a business strategy. Unlike other companies, which primarily use social media for its promotional value, Publitas has recognized the importance of social media in the lives of their clients and their clients' clients. Social media is not only important to the companies that utilize their e-Publishing software, but it is an important part of how those companies do business. The way in which Publitas offers software that is already integrated with social media provides an alternate look at how a company can use social media.

BACKGROUND AND OBJECTIVES

Publitas was founded by Guillermo Sanchez and Khalil Seyedmehdi in 2006. The aim of their company is to enable businesses to convert content to digital formats better. Publitas defines itself as a "professional digital editions application" that allows "professionals and businesses of all sizes to easily create, enrich, publish, and deliver their editions to online and mobile devices." Because their e-Publisher software is cloud-based, users don't have to install any type of software to view online materials. The Publitas software converts print content into a digital format that can be embedded in a Web site, is compatible with RSS distribution, is available for export to offline media such as a USB drive, and can be archived in an online e-library.

Publitas's software, however, allows their clients to do so much more than just convert content into a digital format. Their e-Publisher allows readers to have the best online reading experience due to vector technology for high-quality zooming and automatic pixel resolution. The layout of the online reader facilitates easy navigation through pages and allows readers to do a full text search. Readers have the option to view the content on any number of technological devices. Publitas makes a mobile version so that content is compatible with personal computers, cell phones/smartphones, and digital tablets. Publitas offers clients business-oriented tools through analytics, which allow clients to see statistics about their publications. These statistics include how much time a reader spends on a given page, the resolution at which the publication is being viewed, and the user's browser version. Clients with Google Analytics accounts can also integrate the Google system into Publitas's existing analytics system to receive a more detailed report. Finally, Publitas assists with search engine optimization by incorporating publications into Google's PageRank to drive traffic to a client's Web site.

Not only does this digital format provide a better online reading experience, but Publitas gives their clients control over the content they are releasing. Clients have total control over the aesthetics of their publication with the ability to create unique templates and pick different colors, shapes, and shadows. Clients are also able to choose which features are put into the digital version of their publication and can acquire a personal domain name. Features such as videos, interactive content, and links to digital content enrich the digital experience. New additions to Publitas include the ability to integrate e-commerce directly into a publication. All publications are also compatible across all social media networks for easy content sharing through Facebook, Twitter, etc.

Recently, Publitas has won two awards for their business success. One award, the 2011 Red Herring Top 100 (Europe), selects winners from hundreds of European companies. Companies were judged on their "financial performance, technological innovation, quality of management, execution of strategy, and integration into their respective industries." The other award was the 2011 White Bull Bully Award. Publitas was chosen for its innovation and values of excellence.

ORIGINS

Co-founder Guillermo Sanchez shared the story behind Publitas's founding in an interview. Prior to the conception of Publitas,

Sanchez was working at Deloitte. Having studied computer science in college, he did a lot of work in IT consulting. A college friend who had always been very interested in the Internet and had very creative and innovative tendencies contacted Sanchez. When he shared his idea of an e-publisher with Sanchez, they both quit their jobs to give the idea their full attention.

The company really began with the software that Sanchez's business partner wrote. Sanchez said that Publitas was started in their bedrooms on their personal computers. As he put it, they "bootstrapped the business" and "just jumped in." At this point, their knowledge about the e-publishing market was very limited; they just developed the technology. This might be why their initial foray into the business was met with limited success. The software had been developed with the professional publishing market in mind as a way for publishers to convert their print product into a digital copy that could then be sold. They noticed that most publishers did not have a digital archive of all of their publications and that their software could potentially fill this gap.

Initially, Publitas had a few publishing clients. Sanchez found, however, that it was rather difficult to enter this market because a "digital version of the [same] material would become competition for [the publisher's] own product." Therefore, it was hard for Publitas to convince publishers to convert their products into a format for which there was not necessarily much demand. In 2005, digital tablets had not yet become popular in the same way they have now. They were not as common, as technologically advanced, or as inexpensive as they are today to make them accessible to the majority of people. Because of the obstacle presented by the lack of technological development, digital versions of content were just not a priority for publishers.

BUSINESS DEVELOPMENT PROCESS

Because Publitas was not experiencing the success they had anticipated, Sanchez and his business partner "had to go back to the drawing board." Now that they were more immersed and knowledgeable about e-publishing, they realized that they might have been after the wrong market and that their product might be more successful elsewhere. At this point, Sanchez was much more knowledgeable about e-publishing and now had the experience to make more informed decisions.

Publitas decided to allow retailers to convert their printed catalogs into an online format. Luckily, this market found a much higher value in converting to a digital format, or at least having a digital format of their catalog available to potential consumers. With this shift to the retail market, Publitas started integrating e-commerce into their business model, which Sanchez notes "is a much different direction from the original intent of the company." The technology ultimately developed from a simple reformatting of print content to software that could allow retailers to create a functioning online catalog. Not only is the catalog viewable online, but it is viewable on any number of devices, such as the iPad. The e-commerce integration also allows consumers to treat the digital catalog like the print version and order straight from the product page.

Sanchez also said that they "made a lot of mistakes but were luckily able to correct them." And this correction is what ultimately saved their business. Publitas now holds a market share of 60 percent of operating retailers in the Netherlands. One of their biggest clients, Metro, a German hypermarket company, is one of the top three retail companies worldwide.

SOCIAL MEDIA SOFTWARE INTEGRATION

It was not until Publitas starting extending their business into the retail markets that social media became a central aspect not only of their software but their business practice. As Sanchez explained, "There is no retailer that does not have a social page or that is not active on Twitter. [Consequently], Publitas software allows shoppers to share and interact with content from the catalog and post straight to Twitter. Viewers can then click back to the catalog to create a completely interactive experience with the client's product."

Social media facilitates this cyclical nature of media sharing. Because the Publitas software allows users to share content from the digital catalog directly to a variety of social media outlets, the content then becomes viewable by an even greater number of people. Online catalog viewers can post to social media sites like Twitter, Facebook, LinkedIn, Blogger, StumbleUpon, Tumblr, and Google Bookmarks. In addition to providing an alternate format for a retail company's existing catalog receivers to view, the Publitas software has the ability to extend the company's reach. Sanchez even commented that all of the existing features available to Publitas clients are designed to increase the retailer's reach. Thus, the social media software integration was ultimately shaped by Publitas's change in target markets. The different needs of retailers provided the impetus to integrate social media into their business model and software.

SOCIAL MEDIA STRATEGY

Sanchez admitted that social media for their company's promotion did not necessarily play a huge role until recently. Even though the company dealt with social media in terms of their software, Publitas had not personally been using social media. Due to the company's success with retailers in the Netherlands, Publitas has plans for international expansion into the United Kingdom, Germany, and the United States. They are using social media to facilitate their move into foreign markets. The enterprise companies that Publitas is looking to target have extensive social media use.

The companies Sanchez said Publitas was hoping to secure as clients are very involved in social media for customer service and company promotion purposes. In a conversation with Arka der Stepanian, the director of online marketing at Publitas.com, some light was shed on the ways Publitas is using social media for future goals: "Over the past few months, one of my main tasks here has been to develop a social media strategy to increase our digital footprint and ultimately to generate quality leads."

Currently, Publitas has a Twitter account, a Facebook account, a LinkedIn account, a blog, and a YouTube account. They are the most active on Twitter and Facebook, although activity only started about three months ago when plans for international expansion began. They have 108 followers on their Twitter account and 229 likes on their Facebook page. Sanchez said that their social media strategy is still being established, but that the main focus is to drive traffic to Publitas's Web site. Specifically, Publitas's Twitter account acts as a newsfeed of information relevant to the market. They provide links to content on popular marketing, business, and social media sites such as Mashable.com.

The Facebook page has a similar newsfeed-like quality but also includes links to more Publitas-specific content. One such example is a link to a new clothing catalog for one of Publitas's clients that just went online. Because the focus of Publitas's social media use is to draw in potential clients in the international markets they are breaking into, infographics are readily used to appeal to potential clients. Sanchez said that they like to post infographics that provide relevant information to potential clients, such as people's use of iPads. He feels this is useful because it shows potential clients how Publitas can be useful and relevant to their business.

RELEVANCE OF DIGITAL CONTENT IN THE AGE OF SOCIAL MEDIA

When asked about the way Publitas has changed with the growth in popularity and permeation of social media into both business and social life, Sanchez pointed to the development of technology. In the interview, Sanchez often mentioned the iPad as a primary device for content viewing; however, it has not always been that way. When Publitas first started partnering with retail companies, the retailers told them that paper flyers and catalogs were still effective. At this time, customers were still saying that they wanted the printed material—not everyone wanted the digital version. As Sanchez explained it, "paper [catalogs create] the coffee table or living room moment."

The coffee table or living room moment that Sanchez is referring to is the amount of time that catalog receivers take when they get a catalog to sit down and flip through it—they are sitting on a couch or armchair, not at their desks staring at their computer. It is only recently, however, that research has showed that customers favor digital content over the print version. According to research, on average, catalog receivers look at only nine to ten pages. On a tablet, however, digital catalog receivers look at twenty pages of the digital version.

It is as if Publitas has been waiting for this shift for their entire existence and it is now finally here. Smartphones and digital tablets are now so prevalent that people no longer feel burdened by digital content but rather liberated. Instead of being tied to a desktop computer to view digital content, viewers can now have their coffee table or living room moment with a portable technological device. Publitas further facilitates this moment with software that makes content viewable on any number of devices.

In addition to the compatibility of digital content provided by Publitas that eases a reader's experience, the enhanced features for companies are invaluable as well. To return to the original question of how Publitas has changed due to social media, the growth and spread of technology, such as the digital tablet, among more and more people has ultimately shaped Publitas software. A reciprocal relationship exists between the way people use their technology—to access social media—and the way they would want to interact with a digital catalog. Thus, integrated into the Publitas software is a way for catalog readers to better engage and interact with the content and ultimately post this content to a social media site.

ADVICE FOR OTHERS

When asked what advice he would give to companies looking to begin using social media, Sanchez's main point was "to make sure you get it right." He said, "If you start with social media, there is no other option than to get it right." This attitude is apparent in Publitas's own social media use, in that their strategy has undergone a slow and thought-out development. Because Publitas started using social media only recently, they realized that they had to establish a social media presence before they could reasonably expect results.

Sanchez advises that, with social media, you cannot "expect an immediate and miraculous result." He says "it is really a lot of work to interact with your audience and to post quality content," which makes social media use "a long-term investment." This is an important aspect of social media that I believe many companies overlook; as Sanchez states, "you won't be able to see a direct return on the investment." This issue is due to the way the effects of social media are difficult to discern and quantify. For most companies, improved customer communication, reputation management, and product promotion are goals for a social media campaign. The issue, however, lies in that it is nearly impossible to measure these two goals in terms of social media; a number of other components could be affecting customer service and sales. If social media, however, is "managed right, the return can be exponential."

ING Direct: A Different Kind of Bank

Although recent years have further illustrated why most consumers hate banks, ING Direct USA is enjoying a great relationship with customers who use this virtual bank branch of the European banking giant ING.

ING Direct is certainly not like any other banks. Customers do business exclusively online, over the phone, or by mail. You would think that this would mean a less personalized experience for the user, but it's completely the opposite. The bank has a simple and direct value proposition that its customers appreciate—great and competitive interest rates, 24/7 convenience, and superior customer service. In fact, when you call in and speak to someone, they sound genuinely happy to assist. Word has spread about the friendliness and knowledgeable service. In the United States alone, ING Direct has more than two million customers and growing.

The U.S. branch of this European bank is located in Wilmington, Delaware, with Internet cafés in Philadelphia, New York, Los Angeles, and Wilmington. Its Dutch origins include banking, insurance, and asset management for more than sixty million private, corporate, and institution clients in more than fifty countries. Its long-standing success around the world, which is replicated in its U.S. operations, relies on a simple but very effective set of business objectives, namely efficient use of technology, low-cost model, value focus for the customer, and a simplified and stripped-down operational framework to stay fluid and nimble. This way, the lower costs and simplified approach allow them to provide more value to customers—better interest rates and returns on putting their money with ING, as well as an extensive line of products, including savings, checking, and retirement accounts, as well as mortgages and share purchases.

The company goes out of its way to ensure customers have a great experience, including alleviating fears about working with a bank that is completely virtual. They go so far out of their way that the University of California, Berkeley, rated them as the safest bank in the country in 2008 through a study that looked at identify theft complaints. Then there are the other value-added features that make them stand out from other banks, which are currently under fire for their fees and fees on top of fees that are charged to customers for any type of business they want to do. ING Direct is completely different. They do not charge for bill paying or overdrafts and, most important, for using a debit card. If you need a paper check, they will send it to you. There are no minimum amounts to open a certificate of deposit (CD), and they will reward you with a bonus for refer-ring them to a friend or if you decide to open more accounts with them. The key element in their success is acknowledging just how important their customer is—something that has got-ten lost in how so many companies view their customers and run their businesses. When most banks make you feel as if you are inconveniencing them by working with them, ING Direct thanks you in more ways than one.

However, it's still unknown what impact Capital One's pur-chase will have on the company. The initial reaction by custom-ers was very negative, given that Capital One has not necessarily shown itself to have the same philosophy and approach with their customers. One can only hope that ING Direct remains on the list of success case studies.

Virgin America: The Humble Airline

Unlike the aforementioned players in the airline industry, which seem to be consumed by a certain level of arrogance that clouds their judgment and might be impacting their ser-vice reputation and increasingly troubled bottom line, Virgin America, the latest brand addition to Richard Branson's wildly successful Virgin Group of companies, has already stood out as a success.

Like ING Direct and so many other examples of successful companies, Virgin America is a humble company that under-stands the importance of customers in determining their success and ongoing growth. Every aspect of Virgin America's strat-egy, which is built on the foundation that has led to significant achievements across many of the companies associated with the Virgin brand, is geared toward the customer experience in terms of service, amenities, and everything else that adds value.

From extensive entertainment choices, even on short flights, to low prices and custom and luxurious cabin appointments, Virgin America is beating all the domestic legacy carriers hands down. Most passengers are simply asking Virgin America to add more routes so that they can choose this carrier on every trip they plan. First, there is the entertainment. Even on a short flight, it is great to be amused because it makes time fly. Virgin's in-flight entertainment includes a display where you can order food and drinks, play video games, watch satellite TV, and interact with other passengers. It even comes with a remote that works as a video game controller and has a full keyboard on the back of it.

Then there is the airplane itself. The beaming and stylishly dressed crew members actually seem pleased to welcome you aboard. Virgin America has added some cool decor to what is usually a utilitarian experience. Purple and blue lights line the top of the cabin above sleek leather seats—and those leather seats are even provided for those of you in economy. As soon as you sit down, you are acknowledged by Virgin's interactive screen on the back of the seat in front of you.

Other airlines could learn so much from this carrier and why they are a standout success. They even let the competition know it through their clever marketing slogan: "This is How to Fly." Yes, there are cheaper airlines in terms of the actual flight cost, but when you factor in the service level, amenities, and over-all experience from start to finish, Virgin America is a prime example of what can be done well in a service-oriented industry.

The Handbook on Strategic Evolution: Barnes & Noble

Finally, there is the success story of Barnes & Noble, which serves as a contrast to the downfall of Borders, which was described in the last chapter. This story defines flexibility and strategic evolution as two key traits for success. Overall, Barnes & Noble was able to adapt to this time and age, when people want to do things differently. In contrast, less successful companies simply stick with their initial strategy.

However, very early on, Barnes & Noble developed their Nook philosophy and started actively promoting that. Instead of being afraid that technology might kill their business, they embraced it and figured out how they could turn it into an additional revenue stream by realigning their business model to stay with the trends their target audience was following. Essentially, they took on the challenge Amazon handed them and they delivered by being flexible and adapting their business model to remain relevant.

Many have shared their opinions about what Barnes & Noble has done right and Borders did wrong. These two companies represent polar opposites of how business strategy can be developed and applied:

- Although Borders did not adequately address its Internet sales channel and ignored the e-reader movement, Barnes & Noble reacted swiftly, changing gears to address these two critical trends.
- Barnes & Noble emphasized these strategies rather than focusing on brick-and-mortar stores. That allowed them to avoid becoming enslaved to long leases for locations that performed poorly but could not be closed.
- Despite offering music, movies, games, and other media within their book stores and online, Barnes & Noble did not focus too tightly on one particular diversified segment as Borders did.

- Barnes & Noble created an efficient operational strategy to keep the organization simple so that it could respond nimbly to adjust inventory and offerings when trends among its customer base changed. Unlike Borders, Barnes & Noble has not attempted to be everything to everybody; they are just being what their customer base appears to want after studying them carefully and interacting with them.

- Barnes & Noble invested considerable resources in the 1990s to change their supply chain offerings and inventory-on-hand systems and processes, which reduced labor and time to market and kept costs low.

- In recognizing how much consumers like to linger over magazines and books, Barnes & Noble set up coffee shops within their stores to keep customers there longer and to possibly attract additional customers who might otherwise have only shopped online. They did it smartly by recognizing that consumers like brands. One of their favorites at the time—and even today—was Starbucks. As a result, they pursued and won a contract with this admired and successful brand.

- To attract customers to their physical locations, Barnes & Noble regularly hosts in-store concerts and children's story times, making a trip to the bookstore an experience rather than an errand. This is another way to pull customers away from their computers to shop for what the company offers.

- Finally, Barnes & Noble is led by people who are passionate about the business. Unfortunately for Borders, those who acquired the company and had leadership roles came from "big box" retailers and were not necessarily in love with the product offering in the way book-oriented people are.

LESSONS TO BE LEARNED: TIMING IS EVERYTHING

In looking at these examples, one of the lessons to be learned is that "timing is everything." Timing is a crucial element of why some companies are more successful than others. Though it often combines with other factors, such as chemistry, it's true that without the right timing, you will not reach full potential. Although people often say, "It was not meant to be," what they are truly referring to is timing.

For example, we recently met with another company to discuss a strategic alliance between our two companies. From the start, our conversations ran smoothly and quickly. We came to the conclusion in a minimum amount of time that nothing would prevent us from moving forward together and that we were a perfect fit for one another. The interesting angle of this story is that we had had these same discussions three years earlier. Even then, we felt it might be a good fit and reached the same conclusion just a year and a half ago. However, in both cases, it turned out that we could not progress. At the time, we blamed chemistry. The problem really was that our heads were simply not in it. In both instances, our companies were still developing, so it was clear that we simply were not ready for that kind of step. However, everything has changed at the time of this writing. This other company has adapted to its market and made improvements; E Factor has grown significantly and is now regularly receiving interest about its mentoring and coaching capabilities from members. Voila! Our discussions this time around were simple, purely because both companies were ready for the alliance.

Another thing to remember about timing is never to write off contacts that do not lead to something immediately. I know from experience how hard it is to maintain thousands of casual and business relationships. However, with today's advanced technology like convenient social networking tools and devices that allow you to upload contact information quickly, it's much easier to maintain these potential points of contact for future opportunities. Another way to keep in contact, which we use at E Factor, is to write regular blogs and share the information with all of our contacts. The result of this sharing is active interaction, which leads to interesting exchanges of ideas, as well as new paths to explore. You might also create a newsletter to keep your contacts informed about your activities and adventures. Or simply add them all to your Twitter list so you can use briefer messages to connect from time to time. What you will find over time is that those connections will lead to something valuable—but only when the time is right, of course!

Timing also plays a major role when it comes to raising the funds necessary to start a business or expand operations. This reminds me of when I was invited to invest in a company during the 1980s. The company had developed very impressive 3-D software, which at the time required a roomful of computers to do all of the necessary calculations. However, in my opinion, it was simply not the right time—it would have been much too expensive to be the evangelist to bring something to market at a time when the audience clearly was not educated or informed enough about 3-D to take up the cause. Now of course, thanks to James Cameron, who developed his own 3-D technology with his strategic partners to make the movie *Avatar*, 3-D is now all the rage across so many applications. That is why, if you want to bring something new to the market, you always want to consider if the timing is right and if you have enough money to educate those you are trying to interest, if necessary.

So, if you feel that the timing is not right, you should not force it but simply sit back, stay in touch, and wait until it is right. Again, this is why networking—traditionally and virtually—is such a vital activity for you as an entrepreneur.

MORE LESSONS: THE ART OF THE SALE

Selling is an art. You might know that as an entrepreneur, but you might not fully understand the finer nuances of viewing sales in this way. The managers of today's successful companies fully comprehend the artistic process necessary for sales. Selling is not something you do "in between" other chores or without thought and careful preparation. If you want to excel in sales, it will take a lot of time and a lot of discipline. Let's start from the beginning.

You have an idea for a product or service or maybe you already have moved it to a more finalized state. You want to bring this to the market. The first question you should ask yourself is *Why?* Is it because you like it yourself or because you feel there is a market for it? Did you research whether there are similar products or services? And, if there are, what is their place in the market and how do they position themselves? You can either place your product or service in the same way (which will always cost you a percentage of your margin) or you can give it a twist and make it something new and different and more exclusive. If so, then price will not be the mainstay of your sales process.

Did you consider which industry will be best for your product? And, if so, which segment of that market would you like to enter? It is important to understand that many large corporations have preferred supplier lists and getting onto these could be a long, arduous process. Although they obviously have and spend the money, is this approach really the best way for you to start and, if so, how do you go about it? Or, should you consider a lower, smaller group of companies (midsized) that offer much easier and quicker access?

Once you have chosen your segment, it is worthwhile to speak to a number of potential customers about your intended product/service. Under what terms would they actually consider using your product/service or switching from a competitive one? Answers to these kinds of questions will help you fine-tune and sharpen your selling proposition.

If you have a brand new and unique product/service (and trust me, you should be honest with yourself answering that question!), consider if you have enough working capital lined up to allow you to spend time educating your audience. They need to understand what it is you are selling. They are probably not waiting for your product or service, so it will take quite some time to get them on board. Therefore, you will need to bridge that time period between consideration, interest, and purchase.

Once you do have your product/service, you know how to position it, and you understand your market, then and only then can we really start selling. The whole sales process is a matter of the utmost discipline, and it is a numbers game. Use your time efficiently. For instance, the actual prime selling time you have each day is from 9 A.M. to 6 P.M. Given that it has been scientifically proven that you only use 50 percent of that time effectively, everything that has nothing to do with the actual selling itself, such as drafting proposals, preparing for your calls, and doing your paperwork, needs to be done in the evening or during the weekend. Plan your time efficiently by lining up more than one appointment in any given area you visit. Set aside time in a quiet environment where you can concentrate and not be disturbed every five seconds to call and plan your appointments.

Next, it is all about follow-up, follow-up, follow-up. One of the biggest mistakes we see is that people set an appointment, do the meeting, and then do not respond fast enough. Do not leave it a week or so; follow up with your prospects when the meeting is still fresh in their minds. Use a customer relationship management program to track your process and be disciplined about it. Do not put off a follow-up call or meeting because you are a little worried about it—it's better to know than not to know. You need to figure out and learn how many calls lead to how many meetings lead to how many proposals lead to how many sales. That is the only way to forecast the revenue you will generate each month or quarter accurately. It really works, but you have to understand this process and stick with it to reap the rewards.

KEY POINTS TO REMEMBER

- Early on, successful entrepreneurs realize that they cannot always stick with their original plan. If anything, changing the plan will actually result in bigger and better results than originally anticipated. This means being flexible and willing to evolve strategically and adapt to stay strong and relevant.

- Stay focused more on how to be the best that you can be, which is something that many entrepreneurs and company leaders have not yet learned to do.
- Engage with customers continually to learn from them, research everything, and consult statistics regularly to see where changes need to be made.
- Timing is everything; it's a crucial element of why some companies are more successful than others.
- Selling is not something you do "in between" other chores or without thought and careful preparation. If you want to excel in sales, it will take a lot of your time and a lot of discipline.
- The case studies in this chapter show companies that are willing to change, adapt, be flexible, be open, listen to their customers, interact with their customers and partners, be humble and appreciative, be socially responsible, and imbue all their actions and decisions with the passion they have for their business and what they are doing.

A NEW VISION FOR TODAY'S ENTREPRENEUR

IN LOOKING TO THE future, as an entrepreneur, you have to recognize the importance of collaborating with others like yourself. Unlike traditional businesses, which often rely on the government for assistance, entrepreneurs are an often misunderstood breed. Despite the economic stimulus they have provided, they are frequently underappreciated in the eyes of many country leaders. This chapter provides insights into the future of entrepreneurship, your business, and your opportunities.

DECIDING ON YOUR FUTURE BEFORE GETTING STARTED

When envisioning your future, you must begin before you launch your startup or when your business is in its infancy. Businesses are made up of lifecycles and you must decide which parts of that lifecycle you are effective at and can provide a certain return or positive result. It's likely you are not as effective at other aspects—be honest with yourself, you cannot excel at every component of a business lifecycle—and you might need a strategic partner or some type of assistance. Collaboration and sharing are often necessary.

While you are considering aspects of the lifecycle you are good at—idea, start-up mode, management, growth, or acquisition—you also want to think deeply about what the business means to you. By this, we mean what do you want from it over its lifecycle? Are you someone who simply likes to work as an incubator, coming up with the ideas and then letting someone else take over the management of operations? Is the business for life in terms of generating a monthly income? Do you want to create something that stays on a local scale or grows to international proportions? For each type of scenario and purpose, you must consider the implications, determining an exit strategy at some point in the business lifecycle. For instance, you may want to exit a business-for-life (or lifestyle) model by passing it down to your children. Or you could see it grow organically to be handed off to a successor or be acquired by another company. Maybe you are the one who will be doing the acquiring in order to grow it to international proportions.

One common strategy companies employ—as E Factor has done—is to decide on an initial public offering (IPO). This is the ideal evolution when one wants to grow a business further but needs resources to do so. These resources include money and expertise. By using the shares as a tradeable currency post-IPO to acquire companies instead of (only) using cash, there's no need to wait to take the business to the next level. Typically, waves of consolidation occur within every type of industry in which medium-size players buy up smaller companies, then larger companies turn around and acquire the somewhat larger (but still medium-sized) companies. Then the cycle is repeated as new competition enters the industry when the number of players diminishes during the consolidation phase.

The IPO process is also used as an exit strategy to allow someone better at the next stage in the business lifecycle to take the reins and continue the evolution of the business. It can also be used as a way to reward and repay early investors in the business and allow them to exit within the three to five years they had waited to receive their return. In all respects, it can provide a benefit for the firm and its founders, as well as those willing to buy into the firm through a public offering of company shares. It can also be seen as a collaborative and sharing process through which everyone can benefit if the company can be strategically directed in a way that increases its valuation.

Whatever you decide, the point is that you must first decide before you get too far into the business lifecycle. If anything, you need to know your exit strategy prior to starting, no matter how strange that might sound. Knowing your exit strategy early on helps you choose which pathway you will take as you make decisions about that business. Although this can be a somewhat daunting proposition, it does not have to be, especially if you decide to leverage the support and knowledge of those in similar situations or who have been in similar situations previously.

As an entrepreneur, you will also experience your own life-cycle. Everything in life has a time and place. This is particularly true if you see how your life develops over time. Even if you think you have it all mapped out, you will encounter variables—things that make you realize in hindsight that it was destined to be that way. Such was the case for Adrie.

The most beautiful time for entrepreneurs is generally in their twenties. This is a time of innocence, of learning and experimenting. At that age, you do not have a whole lot to lose and not many obligations. You have the urge to start something for yourself, possibly latent but triggered by one incident. In Adrie's case, he had tried this and that by the age of nineteen but always in addition to a steady job, which turned out to be difficult. You can't start a company without total focus and dedication. When the company he worked for at the time closed down, he did not miss a beat before starting his own company. It was a wonderful time because he learned something new every single day. There were no beaten paths to follow. Every day was new and exciting, partly because he did not come from a family of entrepreneurs and never had an education preparing him to be one. You really do have to have a guardian angel watching over you or you will fail at the first of many, many challenges.

The second part of the lifecycle as Adrie experienced it was between the ages of thirty and forty-five—a period of growth. You have made your first mistakes, learned from them, and survived. Your company now enters a different phase altogether and you have to start looking into things such as accountants or legal personnel. This is the structuring phase of an organization as it slowly becomes less dependent on the founder. Of course, you continue to be the driving force behind the vision, not to mention the billboard for the world beyond the company's walls.

Next, you hit a phase of consolidation and controlled growth or an exit. This is not the most appealing period in my view because it involves hiring and managing groups of people. The first time you do this, it is a massive challenge of course because you want to obtain the maximum results, but you are still learning the jargon and strategies as you sit with attorneys, accountants, and investment bankers and try to talk the talk.

The biggest challenge, however, as you grow older is to understand your own strengths and weaknesses, so that you can work with those who complement you and form a partnership in which you respect and appreciate each other.

GENERATING YOUR OWN STRATEGY . . . TOGETHER

As Adrie's story reminds us, one of the biggest challenges you will face is getting caught up in your own strategy and day-to-day operations rather than tapping into a network of those just like you who can help you address issues and conquer the barriers that stand in your path. Entrepreneurs tend to become very self-focused, but it is actually to their advantage to be more willing to be open to helping one another. However, the winds of change are blowing across many other parts of society, which is making the idea of exchange, interaction, and sharing more amenable to all of us.

In many ways, the social networking framework is changing perspectives about this concept. The popular uprising in Egypt demonstrates how social media makes a huge difference in how people can voice their opinions. This was repeated in many other Arab countries soon afterward, shaking up a number of oppressive regimes. The willingness to share and support one another ultimately paid off because it gave many who had not had the courage to take action the reason and ammunition to do so. For the rest of the world, it opened our eyes to what was previously not known or understood about the plight or feelings of those involved in these conflicts. The new understanding changed perspectives and stimulated a willingness to support those who might have previously been misunderstood or mistrusted.

Although that is a dramatic example, it does illustrate how the same willingness to help one another through that ideal of the community can also aid entrepreneurship. We can achieve a greater understanding about something that was previously unknown or misunderstood—like another entrepreneur, their business model, or their niche idea—which leads to trust and admiration, which in turn stimulates a willingness to help.

Every entrepreneur has a piece of knowledge that can ultimately benefit somebody else. However, to generate the true benefit, you as an entrepreneur have to be willing to share that knowledge. This might mean going out of your way to share with somebody you might not know very well. But, in time, karma will kick in and the benefit of your willingness to share will be returned to you in some form or another.

That is what we have attempted to replicate on a large scale with the E Factor community. Our goal is to become the Facebook of the entrepreneurial landscape. That is why the primary directive of E Factor is not about us telling others how to do things. It is geared toward everyone out there telling everyone else how to do things through a more horizontal, peer-to-peer process. In this way, helping your peers will eventually benefit everybody else to make the dramatic

changes necessary to survive as a species within the evolutionary chain of events.

THOUGHTS ON THE FUTURE

The future is always going to be a challenge, but when you
keep your eyes and ears open, you will better understand what
is going on and why. You can also avoid getting distracted by
the challenges and letting fear prevent you from responding to
ongoing change.

Those of you reading this who represent the future of entrepreneurship or who mentor those who will eventually start
businesses have to recognize that many of the traditional ways
of doing business, including the networking and fund-raising
processes, will be very similar to those of the past. On the other
hand, social media is here to stay, and many new tools are coming out that require you to adapt and be willing to learn how
they can help you. For example, the whole crowdfunding concept is not necessarily a completely new idea, but the regulations that previously inhibited this process are finally changing
to open up its true potential.

The future will also require that you, as entrepreneurs, adopt
a lot of new technology. You'll have to find a way to reach out
to people you do not know—but need to know—and determine
the most appropriate way to present yourself and your company beyond a business plan and a PowerPoint presentation.

You will have to contend with new competition in areas
previously disregarded by past decades of business (again, out
of arrogance and presumption of power). This means facing

countries like India and China, which will be flooding the market with new initiatives and ideas. The world will continue to shrink in terms of business transactions and information exchange. For example, if you came up with an idea about twenty years ago, you could be the only one with that idea for a while. Today and in the future, you see—and will experience—that there are already twenty to thirty companies with more or less the same idea you assumed was yours alone. This fight for idea space will increase dramatically now that China and India are in the game. Entrepreneurs who adapt and prepare for these changes now will be better positioned to address these challenges and thrive as future success stories.

E FACTOR AND THE ONGOING EVOLUTION OF THE SOCIAL NETWORK

As entrepreneurs like you, we have always had our eyes on the future. We have known exactly what our strategy would be for E Factor: become the Facebook of the entrepreneurial world and serve as the strong and silent partner for every entrepreneur out there to allow all of you to improve the quality and quantity of your business. It is a tall order to fulfill, but we are entirely confident it can be done because of what we have built and achieved to date.

Thanks to the social network framework that now influences all of us daily in both work and personal settings, we are operating within a changed landscape, which will continue to be reshaped and redefined by this social network. This new way of working and living has changed how every industry thinks about their customers, partners, and businesses and, in turn, their strategies. Even the companies that ushered us into the social network movement are being influenced by what they created. For example, Facebook is taking very traditional services and rethinking how they can be used within a social network setting. They are packaging them differently and offering them in a more convenient way that only the newer generations behind social networking can visualize. It is an exciting time in which to be thriving as an entrepreneur because you will be part of the ongoing evolutionary change that social networking and social media will initiate.

Consider the information we have shared with you, which we have gathered in collaboration with numerous sources and experiences throughout our forty years as entrepreneurs. Use what you can, but be sure to share what you learn with others like you who are passionate, creative, and driven to create businesses. Collaborate with us as a member of the E Factor community and meet others who can help you and whom you can help in return. In this way, entrepreneurship will continue to build momentum and positive change for all of us.

KEY POINTS TO REMEMBER

- Although the government might not appreciate what you are as an entrepreneur and they might not understand your mindset, they do understand that you can generate jobs, so take advantage of the support they may try to offer.
- Do not feel that you have to go it alone when dealing with barriers and challenges or even when enjoying opportunities and successes. Today's entrepreneur must be willing to be open, to share, to reach out,

and to collaborate with others. This willingness can generate change and create win-wins for all those involved.

- In envisioning the future you would like to have, you must start thinking about what you want before you launch your startup or when your business is in its infancy. Know what you want the future result to be even before you start so you can guide your strategy and decisions in the direction of your exit strategy.

- Although some of you may prefer to stay small and local, others will want to grow to international proportions by acquiring other companies. In this case, you may want to develop an exit strategy around an initial public offering (IPO) to generate the necessary cash flow through shares that you will need to build a bigger business.

- The future is full of even more challenges as competition grows from strong forces like China, India, and Russia, which will be able to come to market fast with a duplicate of your idea at a lower price. You need to be ready to contend with these forces by bolstering your own forces through a tighter support system found within the entrepreneurial community.

- Social networking will continue to lead the evolutionary process in business and entrepreneurship. E Factor will be there to help entrepreneurs as a strong and silent partner, offering the tools and community you need to achieve your passions and dreams.

ACKNOWLEDGMENTS

The development of this book very much mirrors what we intended E Factor, as the world's largest social network for entrepreneurs, to be: It is the result of a collaborative effort between a diverse group of talent and ideas.

We would like to extend our thanks to the following people who were part of the team:

To Roeland, our co-founder and conspirator on all things entrepreneurial.

To Nina Gass for getting what we were trying to achieve with the book, helping us shape it, and delivering excellent work throughout the entire process.

To Jocelyn Reist, our intern, for developing the case studies found within.

To our agent, Raoul Davis of Ascendant Strategy, for guiding us through the process.

To our publisher, BenBella, for expert advice.

To each other for serving as a mentor in various aspects of our life and working as a great team.

Last, but certainly not least, to entrepreneurs around the world without whom we would never have made this journey or been inspired to write this book.

NOTES

1   http://www.nytimes.com/2011/09/22/garden/on-kickstart-er-designers-dreams-materialize.html?pagewanted=all

2   http://www.finextra.com/news/fullstory.aspx?newsitemid=22687; www.symbid.com

3   CNN - Surprise hit 'Paranormal Activity' scares money out of moviegoers: http://www.cnn.com/2009/SHOWBIZ/Movies/10/12/paranormal.activity.movie/index.html

- Social Media Case Study: How a $15,000 horror movie made more than $7 million with help of Twitter and Facebook: http://www.slideshare.net/soravjain/paranormal-activity-social-media-success-case-study
- Paranormal Activity Tries to Ride Social Media Buzz to Wide Release: http://mashable.com/2009/10/07/paranormal-activity/
- Paranormal Activity Rides the Social Web to Millions at the Box Office: http://mashable.com/2009/10/13/paranormal-activity-success/
- San Francisco Chronicle: 'Paranormal Activity' harnessed social media to become a hit movie: http://www.seattlepi.com/movies/411245_paranormal16.html

- Horror Flick Goes Viral…Why Marketing 'Paranormal Activity' via Social Media Made Sense: http://www.wpromote.com/blog/ daily-non-news-stories-of-interest/horror-flick-goes-viralwhy-marketing-paranormal-activity-via-social-media-made-sense/
- MSNBC: Hollywood sees year of 'Paranormal Activity': http://www.msnbc.msn.com/id/35110847/ ns/business-media_biz/
- 'Paranormal Activity' Wins by Listening to Fans' 'Demands': http://adage.com/digitalalist10/ article?article_id=142216
- YouTube Trailer (16,741,131 views): http://www. youtube.com/watch?v=F_UxLEqd074
- Facebook page: http://www.facebook.com/#!/ paranormalactivity?ref=ts
- Entertainment Weekly: Paranormal Activity: A Marketing Campaign So Ingenious It's Scary: http://movie-critics.ew.com/2009/10/07/ paranormal-activity-marketing-campaign/
- AdAge: http://adage.com/madisonandvine/ article?article_id=139588